G000049358

THE WI BOOK OF VEGETABLES AND SALADS

Over 100 recipes tried and tested
by the Women's Institute

MAGGIE BLACK

EBURY
PRESS

ACKNOWLEDGEMENTS

Illustrated by Vanessa Luff
Edited by Suzanne Luchford
Designed by Julia Golding
Cover photography by James Jackson

Published by Ebury Press
Division of The National Magazine Company Limited
Colquhoun House
27–37 Broadwick Street
London W1V 1FR

ISBN 0 85223 600 X

First published 1987

© Copyright 1987 WI Books Ltd

All rights reserved. No part of this publication may be
reproduced, stored in a retrieval system, or transmitted
in any form or by any means, electronic, mechanical,
photocopying, recording, or otherwise without the prior
permission of the copyright owner.

Typeset by Central Southern Typesetters, Eastbourne

Reproduced, printed and bound in Great Britain by
Hazel, Watson & Viney Ltd,
Member of the BPCC Group, Aylesbury, Bucks

CONTENTS

INTRODUCTION

Fresh vegetables are nourishing and full of vitamins minerals and fibres that are essential to our diet. A huge range of home grown and imported vegetables is available. Vegetables are delicious raw or cooked; they give a wonderful variety of colour, flavour and texture.

Choosing fresh vegetables
Where possible use locally-grown vegetables and buy them at their peak, just before they are fully mature. They will be both cheap and plentiful and at their freshest and best, full of nutrients and flavour. Vegetables begin to lose vital vitamin value as soon as they are harvested. Buy unwrapped vegetables if possible, to see just what you are being offered. Refuse any vegetables with discoloured or limp leaves or flesh, with wrinkled skins or with small blemishes which may hide rottenness within.

Storing fresh vegetables
Use all vegetables except main-crop root vegetables as soon as possible. Onions and main-crop root vegetables store well for at least 2 months in a cool, dry dark place; potatoes and carrots, especially, must not be exposed to light. Young and early root vegetables, cabbages and fruits such as pumpkin, courgettes or marrow (if uncut) can be stored for several days in a cool, dry place or for up to 2 weeks in the case of large fruits with tough skins. Most other vegetables should be stored in a cool, dry place or the bottom of a refrigerator for not more than 2–3 days; fragile, tender and leafy vegetables for not more than 1–2 days. Greens such as Brussels sprouts and spinach and any vegetable which has been cut, should be wrapped in a plastic bag or clingfilm before storage. Do not store bean sprouts, kohlrabi, mushrooms, young spinach or sweetcorn cobs.

Preparing fresh vegetables
All vegetables lose vitamins rapidly from any cut surface which is exposed to air and light, so prepare them just before use. In general, leave root vegetables

and fruits unpeeled unless the skins are coarse or blemished and cook them whole or in chunks. However heating, especially in salted cooking liquid, leaches out or destroys nutrients. Vegetables can therefore be cut up finely to shorten the cooking time. Salt should, when possible, only be added after cooking.

Frozen, canned and dried vegetables
Frozen vegetables can be cooked in almost all the ways suggested for fresh vegetables, but will need less cooking time. They are best boiled or steamed without being thawed first. In the case of commercially frozen vegetables, follow the manufacturer's packet directions as to timing, but omit the fat and salt often suggested as additions to the cooking liquid. Frozen vegetables must be thawed and drained before being fried or used in fritters, and most are not suitable for roasting. A few commercially prepared vegetable mixtures are pre-seasoned, but like all vegetables benefit from being flavoured with herbs.

Canned vegetables, well drained, can be used instead of fresh vegetables if necessary and take less time to cook. They are generally canned with salt, and often with sugar or other 'hidden' flavourings, or flavour and colour enhancers.

Freeze dried and other dried vegetables are a useful standby. Follow the packet directions for use but be wary of the quantities suggested; they may be inadequate.

Pulses
Most pulses must be soaked before cooking, and they are then boiled and used as an alternative to potatoes, pasta or rice. A few recipes in this book include cooked, dried beans or lentils; in these cases, canned ones are quite suitable.

Equipment for preparing and cooking vegetables
Hardly any special equipment is needed for preparing and cooking vegetables beyond a sturdy chopping

board, a sharp knife and scissors. A short-bladed knife is easier to use for topping and tailing, scraping and similar tasks. A grapefruit spoon is helpful for removing the seeds from small fruits such as tomatoes. A food processor, blender or powerful food mill is almost essential for making smooth purées, and for very fine chopping and grinding. A steamer or if this is not available, a large, round-bottomed strainer or colander which fits over a saucepan is also useful.

For salad-making, a salad-shaker or basket produces crisp, attractive leaf salads instead of bruised, limp ones; the salad can be drained and shaken in a nylon (not metal) round-bottomed strainer.

All salads should be prepared in a non-metal bowl. A wooden salad bowl is best for serving; it should be wiped dry after use, not washed, to give it the patina and aroma from the dressings used. Always make dressings in a non-metal jug or bowl, or for speed, in a jar or bottle with a firm stopper or screw-on top.

Additional tools such as a large and small vegetable baller, a canelle knife for removing thin strips of peel, and an egg or tomato slicer are also useful. A garlic press saves kitchen smells and washing up.

A healthy diet

It is important to include all the essential nutrients in daily meals, and also dietary fibre and water. Vegetables play a large part in supplying all the components of a healthy diet.

Peas, beans and potatoes provide good protein as well as the starchy carbohydrate which supplies energy. Beetroot contains the most sugar but carrots, onions, parsnips and swedes all contain a higher than average content. Most vegetables contain little or no fat, but avocado pears are rich in it.

Carrots, tomatoes and leaf vegetables all contain carotene which the body can turn into vitamin A and the darker their colour the more they have. Green leaf vegetables are good sources of B vitamins and vitamin C. Raw green salad leaves in spring and summer are especially valuable. Potatoes, green peppers, cabbage and broccoli supply vitamin C year-round. Calcium and iron are also found in green vegetables such as sprouting broccoli, watercress and parsley.

Trim vegetables as little as possible to keep their full fibre value and the nutrients just under the skins of root vegetables. Vitamins and minerals are destroyed by soaking and by over-cooking; cook them as soon as they are prepared, until just tender. *Never* add bicarbonate of soda to cooking water, as it destroys both B vitamins and vitamin C. Season after cooking and serve all vegetables as soon as possible.

Measurements

All spoon measures are level, and eggs are size 3, unless stated otherwise.

Please use either the metric or the imperial measurements; do not mix the two.

American equivalents

	Metric	Imperial	American
Butter, margarine	225 g	8 oz	1 cup
Flour	100 g	4 oz	1 cup
Breadcrumbs, fresh	75 g	3 oz	1¾ cups
Cheese, grated	100 g	4 oz	1¼ cups

An American pint is 16 fl oz compared with the imperial pint of 20 fl oz. A standard American cup measure is considered to hold 8 fl oz.

GENERAL COOKING METHODS AND PREPARATION

A guide to cooking techniques, the preparation
and basic ways of cooking individual vegetables.

To boil

Prepare the vegetables (see page 4) and put them in a pan. Pour on just enough boiling liquid to cover the vegetables; use water, vegetable cooking water or barely seasoned stock. Sprigs of fresh herbs such as mint or parsley can be added. Cook for the time required, topping up with a little extra boiling water if needed. Boil only just long enough to cook, so that the vegetables are tender but retain a slight resistance when bitten. Drain the vegetables thoroughly, reserving any liquid for a gravy, sauce or vegetable soup, season and dress. Serve as soon as possible.

To blanch or parboil

Most vegetables are blanched before freezing, to prevent discolouration or to remove any 'raw' taste before they are used in salads. Sometimes, hard vegetables need parboiling, that is semi-cooking, before being processed by a quick cooking method such as grilling which will complete their cooking.

Prepare the vegetables. To blanch, tip the vegetables into boiling water for a few minutes only. Delicate vegetables should be put in a round-bottomed sieve, colander or frying basket, and just dipped in the water. This will prevent them being squashed when removed.

To parboil, cook the vegetables as for full boiling, but drain them when only partly cooked.

To seal and boil

This is sometimes called the conservation method of boiling because it is designed to retain the nutrients. It is used mainly for root vegetables. The vegetables are cut into small pieces and tossed in a little oil or fat until the surfaces are sealed. They are then cooked in very little liquid – in fact half-steamed – in a covered pan until just tender. Chopped parsley and a dash of lemon juice are usually the only additions after cooking.

To steam
Delicate, young watery vegetables are better steamed than boiled to conserve their nutrients and prevent them becoming sodden. Prepare the vegetables as they will be served, place in the top of a steamer or in a colander and cook, covered, over just bubbling (not fast-boiling) water, until tender. Drain, shaking gently, toss with fresh herbs if used, season and serve.

To bake
Baking is suitable for large vegetables such as Spanish onions or a vegetable marrow, for individual portions of sliced root, bulb or fruit vegetables or for a whole dish of prepared small vegetables such as courgettes or stuffed peppers. Large vegetables are usually baked uncovered with their cut surfaces brushed with fat. Individual portions can be laid on pieces of foil large enough to enclose them, with a light seasoning or a little flavouring liquid. The parcels are then closed; no nutrients are lost because any liquid is served with the vegetables.

To roast
Besides potatoes, onions, parsnips, swedes and pumpkin a few other vegetables can be roasted either round a joint in the oven or in a separate pan. They are generally better if lightly parboiled first, peeled if required, and cooked (topped with fat) at a fairly high temperature to crisp the outside and to cook them quickly. Only roast large chunks or segments of pumpkin; small ones shrivel.

To grill
This method is suitable for mushrooms and halved tomatoes or courgettes. Raw vegetables should be brushed with fat or oil before grilling.

To shallow-fry or sauté

Whole mushrooms, aubergines, courgettes, peppers and similar vegetables, sliced or cut into small cubes or balls, can be tossed in hot fat until just tender and lightly browned. Cooked potato slices can be heated and browned in the same way. Do not leave any vegetable to 'cook itself' in shallow fat; it will absorb too much fat, get soggy and taste greasy. Shallow-fried vegetables should taste crisp.

Finely sliced or cut up vegetables cook in less fat if *stir-fried* in a wok or similar pan; it is an excellent and colourful way to cook mixed vegetables. Cut vegetables into small strips or thin rounds, place the hard ones, and soft ones on separate plates. Heat a few spoonfuls of oil in the pan until hot and toss the harder vegetables in it for a few moments before adding the rest. Stir quickly over a high heat for 2–4 minutes. Add a few spoonfuls of stock, wine or an unthickened spicy sauce. Season well and continue cooking, stirring quickly for a further few minutes, then serve immediately.

A few vegetables with a high water content can simply be cut up and then simmered gently in fat in a covered pan until soft. The pan is shaken often to prevent them sticking. They are tipped out into a serving dish when tender, are seasoned and served with their own liquid.

To deep-fry

The simplest deep-frying method is to slice the vegetables very thinly, dry them well, then immerse them in deep hot oil, 170°C (325°F). The vegetables are cooked until crisp and brown; they are then removed, drained on soft kitchen paper and seasoned with salt.

Alternatively, they can be fried in batter, or egg and breadcrumbs as fritters (for potato chips see page 27).

To braise
Vegetables such as celery, lettuce, fennel and chicory are sometimes braised on a mirepoix of vegetables simmered in fat (see page 66). The mirepoix is covered with stock and the prepared vegetable is laid on top. The pan is tightly covered and the vegetable is cooked very gently, with occasional basting, until tender. Seasoning is not generally necessary.

To purée
All starchy vegetables and a good many others can be puréed for use in soups, as side dishes and as an ingredient of made-up dishes. Boil or steam the vegetables then mash, sieve, or process in a food processor or electric blender. Add a little butter, cream or a thick white sauce or panada (see page 63) and seasoning. Whip with a fork or whisk over a low heat until light and creamy.

Artichokes, globe
Globe artichokes are available all year round. Buy heads with tightly closed leaves, showing no signs of browned or dry edges. There should be no sign of swelling at the base of the artichoke. The bases of the leafy petals are edible and the artichoke bottom or heart is considered a delicacy.

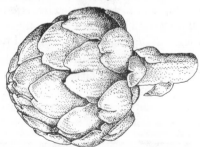

Preparation Break off each stem by bending and twisting it. Remove tough leaves from the base and trim the leaves (optional). If using the bottoms only, remove all the leaves and trim the stem as close as possible to the base. If the artichoke or bottom is to be stuffed, carefully remove the hairy 'choke', pulling it away from the heart with your fingers or scrape it off gently with a knife or spoon. This is easier to do after the basic cooking. Plunge prepared artichoke into cold water sharpened with 1 tablespoon of lemon juice per litre (1¾ pints), to prevent discolouration.

Basic cooking Place the heads in a large pan of boiling water containing a little lemon juice and oil. Cover and simmer for 25–35 minutes for small and medium size heads, 40–55 minutes for large ones. Drain upside down on absorbent paper.

Serve hot with melted butter or hollandaise sauce (see page 65) or cold with a vinaigrette dressing (see page 90).

Artichokes, Jerusalem
These knobbly, white tubers are available from November through to April.

Preparation Wash or scrub the tubers, or peel. If peeling prior to cooking, submerge in cold water with a little lemon juice or vinegar to prevent discolouration.

Basic cooking Boil with just enough water to cover, with a little lemon juice or vinegar added, for about 15–20 minutes until just tender, or steam for about 40 minutes. Drain well and rub or scrape off the skins if necessary. To roast, parboil for 5 minutes, drain, scrape then roast for about 1 hour. To deep fry, parboil for 5 minutes, drain then scrape and cut into slices. Dip in batter and fry until golden brown. Drain on absorbent paper. Thinly sliced peeled raw artichokes, can also be deep fried as for game chips (see page 28). To purée, steam, drain, scrape and cut into pieces. Mash or sieve, season and add 1 tablespoon of butter and milk (optional) for each 450 g (1 lb) of raw artichoke, used.

Asparagus

Asparagus is available all year round. Choose firm, fresh looking stalks.

Preparation Rinse each stalk and cut off any tough and woody ends. Scrape or shave each stalk, if thick, from just below the tip. Trim the stalks to roughly the same lengths and tie into even-sized bundles with the heads together. The spears in each bundle should be the same thickness.

Basic cooking Stand the bundles with the tips upright in a pan at least 5 cm (2 in) deeper than the height of the bundles with enough boiling water to come three-quarters of the way up the stalks. The stalks cook in the boiling water while the tips are steamed. Cover the pan tightly, bring the water back to the boil, and cook gently for 10–20 minutes, until the buds and upper parts of the stems are tender. Drain on absorbent paper and remove the string.

Serve hot with melted butter or hollandaise sauce (see page 65) or cold with a vinaigrette dressing (see page 90).

Aubergines (eggplants)

Aubergines are available all year round. Look for firm smooth aubergines with tight shiny skins. Size makes no difference to the flavour.

Preparation Slice off the stalk and any leaves and wipe or peel. If leaving whole or halved, score or prick the skin in several places. If halved or sliced sprinkle with salt and leave for 30 minutes to remove any bitterness. Rinse thoroughly and pat dry.

Basic cooking Bake whole, or halved and stuffed, in a moderate oven, 180°C (350°F) mark 4, for 30–60 minutes depending on size. Coat slices with flour and shallow fry with squeezed or minced garlic and chopped parsley; or deep fry until golden brown in hot oil, after coating with egg and breadcrumbs.

Avocado pear
Avocados are available all year round. A ripe avocado should be soft and yielding all over.
Preparation Halve avocados lengthways, separate the halves and remove the stone. Brush the cut surfaces with lemon juice immediately to prevent discolouration. Avocados are usually served raw in the shell or sliced in salads.

Bean sprouts
Available all year round. Good with oriental ingredients.
Preparation Rinse lightly. Serve raw in salads.
Basic cooking Steam or stir fry for a few minutes.

Beans, broad
Broad beans are available during the summer. Choose smallish, full but not swollen pods as these are likely to be the youngest and most tender.
Preparation Tiny pods need topping and tailing only. Larger ones should be split and the beans removed.
Basic cooking Cook in boiling water until tender, 15–20 minutes according to age, or steam for 25–40 minutes. Drain well.
Toss with maître d'hôtel butter (see variations, page 67) or hot soured cream.

Beans, French
French beans are available all year, but are best between June and September when home grown. Look for firm, strong beans with a bright green colour. They should break with a crisp snap.
Preparation French beans are usually stringless and only need topping and tailing. Wash.
Basic cooking Boil for 5–12 minutes or steam for about 15 minutes until just tender but still crisp. Drain well.
Season with salt and pepper, toss with a little butter and a few savory or tarragon leaves.

Beans, runner
Available from July to October. Eat very young and
fresh. To test a runner bean for freshness, snap it in
two; it should break with a crisp snap and the inside
should be fresh and juicy. Avoid large, dark green
beans which are likely to be tough and stringy.
Preparation Wash in cold water. Top and tail and
remove strings from the sides of the pod, and slice if
long and thick.
Basic cooking Cook in boiling water for 5–10 minutes or
steam for 15–20 minutes until tender but still crisp.
Drain well.

Toss with a little melted butter and a few savory or
tarragon leaves.

Beetroot
Beetroots are available all year round. Look for firm,
smallish beetroots. The tops, if any, should be crisp
and fresh looking. If buying ready cooked make sure
the skins are not wrinkled or dry, and that any peeled,
prepacked beetroot are glossy.
Preparation Rinse carefully, taking care not to damage
the skin or the colour and flavour will 'bleed' away
during cooking. Twist off the roots about 2.5 cm (1 in)
from the end and trim the tops.
Basic cooking Boil gently until soft, about 30 minutes
for baby beetroots, up to 1½ hours for large ones. To
test if beetroots are cooked, remove one from the pan
and rub the skin gently; it should slide off easily. To
bake beetroots, clean and wrap in foil. If the beetroot is
damaged, 'plaster' the broken skin with flour and
water paste and then wrap in foil. Bake at 180°C
(350°F) mark 4 for 1–2 hours depending on size. The
beetroots are cooked when the flesh yields when
pressed with a finger. Remove the skin.

Slice or dice the beetroot and serve hot with a white
sauce sharpened with a little lemon juice or vinegar, or
chill thoroughly and serve in a salad or with French
dressing (see page 89).

Broccoli – calabrese and sprouting
Green calabrese is available all year round. Cape broccoli is available from February to March. Purple and
white sprouting broccoli are available from February
to March. Buy calabrese and Cape broccoli with a
closely packed head and purple and white sprouting
with strong stalks and heads. All varieties can be used
as for cauliflower in salads (see page 19).
Preparation For purple and white sprouting trim the
stalk and leaves. Prepare calabrese and Cape broccoli
as for cauliflower (see page 19).
Basic cooking Cook purple and white sprouting in boiling water for 6–10 minutes or steam for 15 minutes.
Cook calabrese and Cape broccoli as for cauliflower
(see page 19).
  Serve all varieties with melted butter or hollandaise
sauce (see page 65).

Brussels sprouts
Brussels sprouts are available from August to March.
Choose small, even-sized sprouts that look closely
packed and solid. Avoid any with wilted leaves.
Preparation Wash thoroughly in cold water. Trim off
tough, outer leaves and the stem. Cut a small cross in
the base to help the thick stem cook at the same speed
as the leaves. Shred finely and use raw for salads.
Basic cooking Cook in boiling water or stock for 10–15
minutes or steam for 15–20 minutes. Sprouts can also
be braised as for celery (see page 41). Drain
thoroughly.
  Toss in melted butter or mix with cooked mushrooms, chestnuts or almonds.

Cabbages
Green cabbage is available home grown all year
round. Red cabbage is available home grown from
October to February and imported from September to
June. Spring greens are available home grown
throughout the year. White cabbage is available from

September to June. The most common types of cabbage are spring and summer open-hearted cabbage, spring greens, Savoy cabbage, hard white cabbage and red cabbage. The leaves of green cabbage should be fresh and crisp looking; avoid any that show signs of yellowing. White and red cabbages should be round, closely packed and heavy for their size.

Preparation Discard any damaged leaves. Cut the cabbage into wedges and rinse thoroughly. Cut away the tough stalk. Alternatively, shred the cabbage with a sharp knife, discarding the stalk. Rinse well. Crisp varieties such as Dutch and Savoy make good salad vegetables. Shred finely for coleslaw (see page 72).

Basic cooking Place shredded cabbage in boiling water and cook for 5–10 minutes or steam for 10–15 minutes, until tender but crisp. Cabbage wedges will cook in about 15 minutes. Add 1 tablespoon of vinegar, lemon juice or wine to the water before cooking red cabbage, then boil for 15–20 minutes. Drain well.

Season with salt, pepper and nutmeg and dress with a little melted butter or margarine.

Carrots

Carrots are available all year round. Choose brightly coloured, evenly sized carrots with smooth skins. Avoid soft or shrivelled carrots or hairy, coarse ones.

Preparation For new carrots, top and tail, scrub thoroughly and leave whole. For older carrots, cut a slice from each end and scrape or peel thinly – slice, dice or cut lengthways into quarters or matchsticks. Remove the core if it is woody. Grate young, raw carrots for salads.

Basic cooking Cook in boiling water for 8–10 minutes if sliced or diced, or 10–20 minutes if whole or quartered. Alternatively, steam for 20–25 minutes. Drain well.

Toss in melted butter and sprinkle with fresh herbs. Purée very large carrots or use for soup.

Cauliflower
Cauliflowers are available all year round. Look for fresh green leaves surrounding a firm white head free of blemishes. The curd should be closely packed.
Preparation Cut away the green outside leaves. Cut the stalk level with the head and cut a cross in the end. Cut away any damaged parts of the head and wash thoroughly. Alternatively, cut the head into florets, discarding the centre stalk.
Basic cooking Cook a whole cauliflower stalk down in 2–5 cm (1–2 in) boiling water for about 15–20 minutes, until the stalk is tender but still firm. Cook florets for 5–15 minutes, and drain thoroughly.
　　Serve with butter, white sauce or cheese sauce.

Celeriac
Available from September to March, celeriac has a rich celery flavour and nutty texture.
Preparation Peel and toss in lemon juice or vinaigrette to prevent discolouration. Cut in dice or matchstick pieces or shred. For salads, grate, shred or dice and marinate in dressing to soften, or blanch; or serve grated with a mustard mayonnaise.
Basic cooking Cook in gently boiling water for up to 5 minutes if diced or 1 minute if shredded. Celeriac can also be steamed. Drain.
　　Serve hot with butter, white sauce or hollandaise sauce (see page 65), or make into a purée.

Celery
Celery is available all year round. Look for crisp whole heads with small inner stalks and 'heart'. Avoid over-large heads as they may be stringy. Winter celery has a sweet flavour and tender stalks.
Preparation Trim leaves and roots. Separate stalks and scrub well. String if required. Cut into 2.5 cm (1 in) lengths or leave whole. Use raw, chopped celery in salads.

Basic cooking Cook sliced celery in butter for 5 minutes, add stock, cover and simmer for 15–20 minutes until the stalks are tender but still crisp. Alternatively steam for 20–30 minutes until soft. Drain well.

Serve hot with herbs or cheese sauce.

Chicory
Chicory is available all year round. Look for compact heads, with white leaves and yellow-green edges. Those with green tips will probably be too bitter for salads.

Preparation Wash in cold water if necessary and trim the root end and any damaged leaves. Remove the bitter centre core. Separate each leaf or leave the head whole and quarter or slice it lengthways. Use the leaves raw in salads.

Basic cooking Blanch the whole heads in boiling water for 5 minutes and drain well. Cook in a very little fresh water with lemon juice and a little butter for 20–30 minutes until just tender. Season well.

Serve hot with chopped parsley or paprika or in a white or cheese sauce.

Chillies
Available all year round. Green-skinned chillies are less hot than the red ones.

Preparation Trim off the stalk, wipe and use whole, or chop very finely. If cut, remove all the fiery hot seeds. Wash your hands after handling them.

Add chillies to pickles, curries, stews and hot or cold bean dishes.

Chinese leaves
Available from June to April. The head should be pale green, solid and heavy.

Preparation Wash and dry; shred finely for use raw in salads or halve, quarter or cut into wedges for cooking.

Basic cooking Cook shredded leaves in a little boiling water for 2–3 minutes until tender, yet crisp, or steam for 4 minutes. Boil wedges for 7–10 minutes. Do not overcook. Drain well.

Serve hot sprinkled with herbs and lemon juice or French dressing. Chinese leaves can also be braised.

Courgettes (green and yellow) and small round squashes

Courgettes are available all year round, but are cheaper in summer when squashes can also be bought. Look for medium-sized courgettes with blemish-free skins as the larger ones tend to have tough skins. Courgettes are good raw, in salads.

Preparation Wash or wipe, top and tail. Cook whole, halve or quarter lengthways or cut into rounds. Do not peel unless the skins are tough. Young courgettes can be coarsely grated for use raw or stir fried. Cook squashes whole or halved.

Basic cooking Steam whole courgettes for 10–20 minutes, or boil for the same time, until they are just tender. Cook slices in a little butter or oil in a covered pan for 5 minutes, and season well with salt, black pepper and a few drops of lemon juice. (Halved courgettes or squashes can be stuffed.)

Serve hot with maître d'hôtel butter (see variations, page 67), or cold with yoghurt dressing.

Cucumber

Cucumbers are available all year round. Choose smallish, smooth skinned cucumbers as larger ones tend to be less tender, with bitter indigestible seeds and rather tough skins.

Preparation Wipe, cut off the ends, and cut into slices, dice or chunk. Peel if the skins are tough. Cucumber is usually eaten raw as a salad vegetable, but can also double for cooked courgettes.

Basic cooking Steam or boil for 3–10 minutes depending on sizes of pieces and drain, or sauté in butter for 3–10 minutes.

Serve hot tossed in butter with spring onion and herbs, or cold in a vinaigrette or yoghurt dressing.

Fennel

Imported Florence fennel bulbs are available year round. Select white or pale green, as dark green ones are likely to be rather bitter. Fennel has a crisp texture and a delicate aniseed flavour.

Preparation Trim off the root end and stalks, reserving any feathery leaves to use as a garnish. Remove the coarse outer sheaths of a larger bulb. Either leave the bulb whole, quarter it or slice thinly. Drop cut fennel in water sharpened with a little lemon juice to prevent discolouration. Use raw, thinly sliced fennel in salads.

Basic cooking Blanch whole, small fennel in boiling water for 5 minutes. Put whole or cut fennel into simmering water with lemon juice, or into chicken stock and cook gently for 10–15 minutes if sliced, 25–40 minutes if quartered or whole, depending on size. Alternatively, blanch the whole heads briefly in boiling water, drain and sauté in butter for 5–10 minutes until golden.

Serve hot tossed in melted butter. Serve raw as part of a crudité platter or green salad.

Kale

Kale is available from September to March. The leaves should be fresh and crisp looking.

Preparation Wash and discard any damaged leaves. Use blanched in salads.

Basic cooking Cook in boiling water for about 8 minutes. Drain and season.

Serve hot tossed in butter.

Kohlrabi

Available from July to March. Look for young, small kohlrabi as old ones are tough and bitter.

Preparation Cut off the leaves and stalks. Peel thinly, cut into slices or cubes, or grate for serving raw.

Basic cooking Cook in boiling water for 10–15 minutes until tender.

Serve hot in a white or cheese sauce (see page 64), or

as a purée. Toss grated raw kohlrabi in French dressing (see page 89).

Leeks

Leeks are available from August to April. Look for small, tender leeks, well blanched at the root end and with crisp green tops. Finely sliced, leek stems are delicious raw in salads imparting a mild onion flavour. *Preparation* Cut off the root and any coarse leaves. Cut a lengthways slit nearly half way through the leeks or cut very large leeks lengthways in half and wash thoroughly. Alternatively, slice and wash in a colander. *Basic cooking* Steam sliced leeks for 5–7 minutes, or cook in boiling water for 20 minutes if whole or 5 minutes if sliced. Drain well.

Serve raw, thinly sliced and tossed in French dressing. Serve hot with white or cheese sauce (see page 64) or glazed with maître d'hôtel butter (see variations, page 67).

Lettuce, endive and other salad leaves

Cos lettuce is available from April to October, Iceberg and round or cabbage lettuce and endive and sorrel all year round. Crisp, firm-hearted varieties of lettuce have more flavour than the soft-leaved round lettuce. Look for fresh strong leaves without brown or damaged patches. The endive family includes curly endive, with a slightly bitter flour, patvia chicory and radiccio, Dandelion leaves, corn salad, purslane, mustard and cress, sorrel and watercress can also be used. *Preparation* Wash the leaves and drain well, pat dry or shake well in a salad basket. Trim off any tough ribs or leaves. Keep covered in the refrigerator to retain crispness. *Basic cooking* Lettuce wedges or small whole lettuce can be blanched and then braised until tender (see page 12). Crisp lettuce leaves are good sautéed in butter or oil for 2–3 minutes, stirring all the time, until they just begin to soften. Sorrel can be cooked as for spinach (see page 30).

Toss raw whole or shredded leaves in a herb-flavoured dressing.

Marrow

Marrows are available from June to September. Look for marrows that weigh only about 1 kg (2¼ lb). Large marrows tend to be flavourless and fibrous.

Preparation Peel marrows thinly, scoop out the seeds and cut into chunks or slices.

Basic cooking Steam for 10–25 minutes according to age, drain thoroughly, or sauté in a little butter for 5–10 minutes.

Serve with melted butter and chopped parsley in a coating of white or cream sauce, or cheese sauce (see pages 63 and 64). Marrow is very good split in half and stuffed (see page 56).

Mushrooms

Cultivated mushrooms are available all year round, field mushrooms in September. Look for button mushrooms when appearance is important. For flavour, buy flat or field mushrooms. Eat as soon as possible after purchase.

Preparation Wipe with a damp cloth if necessary; do not peel unless the skin is damaged. Trim off any earthy root. Fresh, raw mushrooms are an excellent source of texture and flavour for salads.

Basic cooking Poach in a little water and lemon juice for 3–5 minutes, drain well. Steam whole or sliced mushrooms for 5–10 minutes until tender. Grill flat mushrooms, brushed both sides with melted butter or margarine and seasoned with salt and pepper, for about 3 minutes on either side. Fry gill side up, in a little butter for 4–6 minutes until tender.

Serve in a cream sauce (see page 63), or sprinkled with chopped parsley or fresh thyme.

Mustard and cress

Mustard and cress is available all year round.

Preparation Wash, cut and serve as part of a salad or as a garnish.

Okra
Imported okra is available all year round. The ribbed pods are best when no more than about 7.5–10 cm (3–4 in) long. A brown tinge indicates staleness so look for clean, dark green pods.
Preparation Rinse, top and tail the pods without cutting into the flesh if cooking whole. If the ridges look tough or damaged, scrape them. Slice or leave whole.
Basic cooking Cook in boiling water for 5 minutes or parboil and finish by tossing in butter, or sauté in oil for 5–10 minutes until tender.

Onions
Large onions and spring onions are available all year round. Pickling onions are available from September to December and shallots from June to July. Look for clean, firm onions with dry, papery skins.
Preparation Cut a thin slice off the top of the onion. Remove the dry papery skin and peel off any soft outer layers. Hold the onion by the root and slice, or cut in half and chop. Discard the root. Spring onions are usually served raw in salads; the green leaves can be chopped and used for flavouring and garnishing. Use shallots raw or cooked like onions.
Basic cooking Cook large onions, with their skins on to preserve the nutrients, in boiling water for 20–50 minutes, depending on size. Drain well. Strip off the wet skin. Steam whole onions for 40 minutes and sliced onions for 15 minutes. Shallow fry thinly sliced onion in enough fat to coat the bottom of the pan for 5–8 minutes until browned, turning occasionally. Drain well. Deep fry thinly sliced, floured onion rings until browned. To bake, parboil with the skin on for 20 minutes (optional) drain and dry. Wrap each onion in greased greaseproof paper, place in a greased baking

tin and bake at 180°C (350°F) mark 4 or at 200°C (400°F) mark 6 if not parboiled until tender, about 45–70 minutes. Remove the skin.

Serve boiled onions with white or cheese sauce (see pages 63 and 64), and baked onions with melted butter.

Parsnips
Available from September to April. Young parsnips are the most tender and the flavour is best after several frosts. Look for firm, clean roots without side shoots or soft brown blemishes.
Preparation Scrub well. Trim the top and end root and peel thinly. Leave whole, slice or quarter as required. Cut out the core from older coarser parsnips.
Basic cooking Steam sliced parsnips for 10 minutes. Parsnip quarters may be blanched in boiling water for 1–2 minutes, drained well and either sautéed or roasted around a joint of meat. To sauté, cook in melted butter for 10–12 minutes until golden and tender. To roast, place in the roasting tin around the joint of meat and cook at 200°C (400°F) mark 6 for about 40 minutes.

Serve with butter or margarine, or as a purée (see page 45).

Peas
Peas are available from March to November and mangetout all year round. Peas should have crisp, young, well-filled pods, with a little air space left between the individual peas. Overfull pods may give tough, hard peas. Home or locally grown ones are often the best because they are more likely to be freshly picked. Mangetout should be eaten as soon as possible after picking. They are eaten whole before the peas start to swell in the pod.
Preparation Shell the peas, discarding any that are blemished or discoloured and wash in running cold water. Use fresh peas as soon as they are shelled, or cover with washed pods if not used immediately; they lose their flavour if soaked. For mangetout rinse the

pods and trim the ends. Mangetout can be eaten raw in salads.

Basic cooking Cook peas in boiling water, with a sprig of mint and 1 teaspoon of sugar, for 5–15 minutes or until just tender. Drain well. Steam mangetout for about 5 minutes, stir fry or sauté gently in butter.

Season and toss in melted butter.

Peppers – green, red and yellow
Imported peppers are available all year round. Look for firm, shiny peppers. The flavour of green peppers is sharper than that of red and yellow peppers.

Preparation Rinse under cold running water, slice off the stem end and take out the core, seeds and inside ribs. Cut into slices or rings. Alternatively, grill until the skins blacken and blister, then rub the skins off. Slices of crisp-textured and strong flavoured raw pepper make colourful additions to salads.

Basic cooking Steam whole peppers for 12 minutes, or stuff and bake whole or halved (see page 58).

Potatoes
Different varieties of potato are available all year round. New potatoes are in season in summer. Sweet potatoes are available from September to June. Look for smooth, evenly sized, firm potatoes, free of blemishes. New potatoes should have skins so soft they will rub off with your thumb.

Preparation Scrub new potatoes; scrub then cut off any scabbed or discoloured parts of old or sweet potatoes, and gouge out any 'eyes'. Peel if to be cooked in slices or roasted. Cut large potatoes into even pieces, or scrub potatoes and cook them in their skins. Either eat the potatoes in their skins, which contain most of the goodness, or peel them after cooking. For deep frying, cut peeled, raw potatoes so that they are 7.5 × 1 cm (3 × ½ in) square for chips, and 5 cm × 5 mm (2 × ¼ in) for French fries. Soak the sticks in cold water for 30–45 minutes to remove excess starch. For baked potatoes, choose those of equal size and scrub. Prick

with a fork and brush with oil. For game chips or
potato crisps cut raw, peeled potatoes into very thin
rounds. Rinse well and dry.

Basic cooking Cook new potatoes in boiling water for
15 minutes and old potatoes for 25–30 minutes. Drain
well. New potatoes are delicious steamed for 20–25
minutes. For roast potatoes, parboil for 5–7 minutes
and roast with the fat round the meat at 220°C (425°F)
mark 7 for 40–50 minutes, turning half-way through.
To shallow fry or sauté, boil until just cooked, slice into
5 mm (¼ in) rounds and cook gently in a little hot fat,
until lightly browned on both sides. Drain on absorbent paper. To deep fry, heat the oil to 190°C (375°F).
Quarter fill the basket with chips and lower into the oil.
Cook until light gold in colour. Drain on absorbent
paper. Repeat with the remaining chips. Reheat the oil
and fry all the chips until crisp and golden. Drain well
and sprinkle with salt. Place baking potatoes in the
oven at 200°C (400°F) mark 6 for 45-55 minutes. For
game chips, fry thin slices until golden brown. Sweet
potatoes can be baked, boiled or parboiled and then
sautéed.

Serve boiled and steamed potatoes with melted
butter. For creamed potatoes, mash with a fork or
potato masher and beat in seasoning, butter and a
little milk or single cream. Reheat gently, beating until
fluffy. For baked potatoes, make a small cross-cut in
the top of each potato and put a dab of butter,
margarine or a little soured cream on top.

Pumpkin
Pumpkin is available from June to January.
Preparation Wash and peel. Cut into wedges or 5 cm
(2 in) chunks.
Basic cooking Roast with a little butter and lemon juice
for 1–2 hours, or steam for 35–40 minutes.

Serve with a little melted butter and chopped parsley
if steamed.

Radishes
Radishes are available all year round. Look for firm, brightly coloured radishes, free from blemishes. Red is the most common colour, but yellow, white and black varieties are available.
Preparation Cut off any stalk or leaves and trim the roots. Wash in cold water. Radishes are usually eaten raw.
Basic cooking Cook in boiling water for 5–10 minutes, according to size. Drain.

Mix cooked radishes with other root vegetables in melted butter and parsley. Use raw radishes sliced, or grated in salads.

Salsify and scorzonera
Available from October to March. These are long thin roots like parsnip; salsify is white and scorzonera black. Salsify is often known as the 'oyster plant' because of its distinctive flavour. Do not scrape or peel scorzonera as the flavour is mainly skin deep.
Preparation Scrub either root carefully and cut into 5 cm (2 in) lengths. Both shrivel and discolour when exposed to air so use immediately.
Basic cooking Put in boiling water sharpened with lemon juice and cook for about 30 minutes until tender. Drain

Season and sprinkle lightly with melted maître d'hôtel butter (see variations, page 67) or in a white sauce (see page 63). Cooled, cooked salsify can be served in French dressing as a salad.

Sea kale
Available from December to May.
Preparation Wash and cut stems into short lengths.
Basic cooking Boil leaves and stems for 15 minutes until just tender, or steam for 10–20 minutes. Drain well.

Serve with hollandaise sauce (see page 65) or melted butter.

Spinach

Spinach is in season all year round. Look for bright green, tender leaves. Avoid spinach that is yellow or wilted. Buy plenty as spinach reduces greatly during cooking.

Preparation Wash well with several changes of water to remove all the grit. For winter or perpetual spinach, remove coarser stalks and centre ribs. For summer spinach, trim the base and stalks and keep the leaves whole. Raw, young spinach leaves make a delicious salad.

Basic cooking Bring 5 mm (¼ in) water to simmering point. Put in the wet leaves and cook gently for 5–10 minutes until limp and tender. Drain, pressing out excess water. Steam for 5–10 minutes in the water that remains on the leaves after washing. Coarser spinach may take a little longer. Drain well.

Season and dress hot spinach with melted butter, or finely chop the leaves, dress with a little hot cream and season with salt, black pepper and nutmeg.

Swedes

Swedes are available from September to May. Select smaller swedes where possible, avoiding those that have been damaged during lifting.

Preparation Scrub and peel swedes to remove all the tough skin and roots. Cut into equal-sized pieces or slices and keep covered in water as swedes discolour quickly.

Basic cooking Cook in boiling water for 30 minutes until tender. Alternatively, steam for 35–40 minutes. Drain well. Swedes can also be mashed, roasted and puréed.

Season with black pepper.

Sweetcorn

Sweetcorn is available from July to October and from February to April. Choose medium-sized cobs with leaves wrapped tightly round them. When the leaves are parted the corn kernels should show plump and very pale yellow; they should exude a milky liquid when dented with a thumbnail.

Preparation Cut off the stalks and remove the outer leaves and 'silk'.

Basic cooking Place some of the husks in a large pan, with the cobs on top. Cover with boiling water and cook for 5–15 minutes depending on age, until a kernel lifts off the cob easily. Drain well.

Serve at once with salt, black pepper and melted butter. If the cobs are very young, the kernels can be scraped off with a sharp knife, slicing downwards towards the stem end.

Swiss chard
A nutritious vegetable available from September to May. Choose fresh-looking crisp stalks and clean dark leaves.

Preparation Prepare and use the stalks, raw or cooked, as for celery (see page 19). Wash and treat the leaves like spinach (see opposite).

Basic cooking Cook the stalks in all the same ways as celery. Cook the leaves like spinach, but season less strongly.

Serve tossed in a little melted butter.

Tomatoes
Tomatoes are available all year round, but they are best from late spring to autumn. Look for firm, un-blemished, light red tomatoes. Dark red tomatoes may be over-ripe.

Preparation Wash, wipe dry and remove the calyx and any stem. Halve, slice or cut into wedges as required. To skin a tomato, dip in boiling water for 1–2 minutes and then plunge into cold water. Strip off the skin from the stem end. Use raw or cooked.

Basic cooking Halve tomatoes and fry in hot oil for 3–5 minutes, turning once. Grill with a dab of fat on top of the cut side of each half for 5–10 minutes depending on thickness. To bake tomatoes, cut a cross in one end, top with a little butter and seasoning and bake at 180°C (350°F) mark 4 for 10–20 minutes depending on size.

Turnips

Turnips are available all year round. Look for turnips with clean, unblemished skins. Buy tender, early turnips with pale green skins in spring and early summer. Main crop turnips are less tender, with creamy coloured skins.

Preparation Trim early turnips and peel thinly for eating raw; leave the skins on for cooking. Peel main crop turnips thickly and cut into pieces or slices before cooking. Cook immediately as they discolour rapidly.

Basic cooking Cook early turnips whole in boiling water for 20–30 minutes, drain and rub off the skins. Cook prepared main crop turnips in boiling water for 15–25 minutes depending on size. Drain well. Turnips may also be cut into large dice and steamed for 15 minutes.

Toss early turnips in melted butter or coat in cheese sauce (see page 64). Main crop turnips can be mashed with milk and butter, or puréed (see page 12).

Watercress

Watercress is available all year round. It should be crisp, fresh and free from discoloured leaves.

Preparation Trim and wash well and serve as part of a salad or as a garnish.

VEGETABLES

VEGETABLES AS ACCOMPANIMENTS

A range of dishes using both common and unusual vegetables.

MACEDOINE OF VEGETABLES

1 turnip
100 g (4 oz) carrots
a few runner beans
225 g (8 oz) shelled peas
a few cauliflower florets
225 g (8 oz) potatoes
850 ml (1½ pints) water
½ tsp salt
2-3 tbsp butter or margarine, melted
chopped parsley to garnish

Prepare all the vegetables, and string, scrape or peel if needed. (Peel potatoes for this dish.) Cut the turnip, carrot and potato into 1 cm (½ in) dice and cut the beans into short lengths. Bring the water to the boil in a pan and add the turnip and carrot. Boil for 3 minutes. Add the beans and boil for 2 minutes more. Add the peas and cauliflower and finally the potato. Cook until the vegetables are tender but not broken or mushy. Drain (keep the cooking liquid for soup). Season, toss in butter and sprinkle with parsley.

A macedoine can also be served cold in mayonnaise. Omit the tossing in butter.

Mixed vegetables cut in small pieces make a colourful border or garnish for meat or other vegetable dishes.

HERBED GREEN BEANS

Serves 4

450-675 g (1-1½ lb) green beans
(French or runner)
2-3 tsp chopped parsley
2-3 tsp finely chopped chives, or
2-3 tbsp finely chopped onion
salt and pepper
lemon juice
50-75 g (2-3 oz) herb butter
(see variations, page 67)

Top, tail and string the beans. Slice runner beans diagonally. Cook the beans, parsley and chives or onion in the minimum of boiling water until tender but still slightly crisp (small thin beans, 5–10 minutes, larger beans about 15 minutes). Drain well. Add a light seasoning of salt and pepper, a few drops of lemon juice and the herb butter in small portions. Toss to coat the beans with some of the butter. Serve in a warmed dish.

If available, use thyme, savory or hyssop leaves for the herb butter.

POLISH BROAD BEANS

Serves 4

450-675 g (1-1½ lb) broad beans,
* shelled*
water or vegetable stock (see page 65)
salt and pepper
2 tsp clear honey
1 tsp French Dijon mustard
150 ml (¼ pint) soured cream or
* natural yoghurt*

Cook the beans in the minimum of boiling water or stock until just tender (12–15 minutes for very small beans, 20–30 minutes for large ones). Drain well and season lightly. Mix the honey and mustard with the cream or yoghurt and add to the beans. Stir over a very low heat, without boiling, until heated through.

FRENCH BEANS SOUBISE

Serves 4

450 g (1 lb) French beans
3 tbsp butter or margarine
12 large or 16 small spring onion bulbs,
* trimmed and sliced*
juice of ½ lemon
salt and pepper

Top, tail and string the beans and boil or steam until just tender. Meanwhile, melt half the butter in a pan, add the sliced onions and simmer until soft. Drain the beans when ready, toss with the remaining butter, lemon juice and seasoning to taste, and sprinkle with the onions.

GLAZED BROCCOLI

Serves 4

4 large or 8 small broccoli spears
3 small onions about 50 g (2 oz) each
3-4 small inside celery stalks
275 ml (½ pint) brown vegetable stock
(see page 66)
gravy browning
12-16 small strips of sweet red pepper

Cut the stems off the broccoli to within 2 cm (¾ in) of the head. Slice the onions and celery thinly. Bring the stock to the boil in a pan with a few drops of gravy browning if it is pale. Add the broccoli, onion and celery and cook gently for 10–15 minutes or until the broccoli and celery are tender. Add a little extra stock if the liquid begins to dry out. At the end of the cooking time, it should be reduced to a syrupy glaze. Add the strips of pepper about 5 minutes before the end of the cooking time.

Lift out the broccoli and place in a well-warmed dish. Arrange the flowers close together and tip the onions, celery and glaze over them. Top the dish with the shreds of pepper.

BRUSSELS SPROUTS AND CHESTNUTS

Serves 4

350 g (12 oz) chestnuts
brown vegetable stock (see page 66)
1 stalk celery, chopped
1 tsp sugar
675 g (1½ lb) Brussels sprouts
salt and freshly ground black pepper
butter for dressing

Prepare the chestnuts by slitting the rounded sides of the outer skins. Put the nuts into cold water and bring to the boil. Drain and remove both the outer and inside skins. Halve or quarter any large nuts. Return to the pan, just cover with stock and add the celery. Simmer gently until the nuts are tender, about 20–35 minutes. Cook the sprouts in the minimum of boiling water for 8–10 minutes. Drain, and return to the dry pan with the chestnuts. Season well with salt and black pepper and toss with butter.

GLAZED BRUSSELS SPROUTS

Serves 4

450 g (1 lb) Brussels sprouts
100 g (4 oz) button mushrooms
40 g (1½ oz) butter or margarine
salt and pepper
grated nutmeg
2 small onions, sliced into thin rings

Boil the Brussels sprouts in the minimum of water until tender (8–10 minutes). Meanwhile, halve the mushrooms, or quarter them if large. Drain the sprouts when ready and set to one side.

Melt 25 g (1 oz) of the butter in a frying pan big enough to hold the sprouts in one layer. Add the mushrooms, and sauté them for 2 minutes. Add the sprouts, and fry turning them over, for 4–5 minutes or until the sprouts are glazed and shiny and the mushrooms are tender. Season well with salt, pepper and nutmeg and transfer to a warmed, shallow serving dish, keep warm.

Add the remaining butter and the onion rings to the pan, and fry quickly until lightly browned. Spread them over the sprouts and mushrooms.

Serve with roast meats or boiled ham.

SCALLOPED WHITE CABBAGE

Serves 4

1 small white cabbage, finely shredded
1 small onion, grated
275 ml (½ pint) boiling water
20 g (¾ oz) butter or margarine
2 level tbsp flour
150 ml (¼ pint) milk
75 g (3 oz) grated cheese
salt and pepper
grated nutmeg

Boil the cabbage and onion in about 275 ml (½ pint) water for 5–8 minutes until tender. Drain, reserving the liquid. Put the cabbage in a greased oven-proof dish. Make a white sauce (see pages 63 and 64) with the butter, flour, milk and 150 ml (¼ pint) of the reserved liquid. Reserve 2 tablespoons of the cheese and stir the rest into the sauce with the seasonings over a gentle heat. When the cheese melts, mix the sauce with the cabbage. Sprinkle with the reserved cheese and place under the grill to brown.

CASSEROLED RED CABBAGE

Serves 6

*2 medium-sized onions, skinned and
sliced*
*25 g (1 oz) bacon fat, dripping or
margarine*
*1 kg (2¼ lb) red cabbage, finely
shredded*
*350 g (12 oz) cooking apples, peeled,
cored and sliced*
2 tbsp golden syrup
salt and ground black pepper
2 tbsp red wine vinegar
2 tbsp water
juice of ½ lemon

Fry the onions in the bacon fat until lightly
browned. Layer the cabbage in a large
casserole with the onions and the frying fat, the
apples, syrup and seasoning. Pour over the
vinegar, water and lemon juice. Cover tightly,
and cook on the stove over a low heat, or in the
oven at 180°C (350°F) mark 4 for 1½ hours.

The cabbage reheats perfectly or can be
used cold instead of pickled red cabbage.

CABBAGE AND MUSHROOM CRUMBLE

Serves 4

450 g (1 lb) firm-hearted green cabbage
3 tbsp margarine
1 tbsp clear honey
1 tbsp lemon juice
salt and black pepper
175 g (6 oz) button mushrooms
pinch of grated nutmeg
*soft breadcrumbs from 2 wholemeal
bread slices*
25 g (1 oz) salted peanuts, chopped
melted margarine

Shred the cabbage, removing the core and any
hard ribs. Melt the margarine in a pan and toss
the cabbage in it over a moderate heat for
1 minute. Add the honey, lemon juice, a little
seasoning and 4 tablespoons water. Reduce the
heat, cover, and simmer gently for 10 minutes,
stirring twice during cooking. Meanwhile slice
the mushrooms and cook in a little water
sharpened with lemon juice for 3 minutes,
then drain and sprinkle with nutmeg.

Spread half the cabbage in a shallow 18-cm
(7-in) baking dish. Spread the mushrooms
over it then top them evenly with the rest of the
cabbage. Mix the breadcrumbs and peanuts
and scatter them over the top. Sprinkle with
melted margarine and put under the grill to
brown.

VICHY CARROTS

Serves 4

450 g (1 lb) carrots
425 ml (3/4 pint) water
pinch of salt
3 tbsp butter
1 tsp sugar
freshly ground pepper
chopped parsley to garnish

Slice old carrots but leave young 'baby' carrots whole. Blanch old carrots in boiling water for 2 minutes, then drain. Return the carrots to the pan with the measured water, salt, 1 tablespoon of the butter and the sugar. Bring to the boil, and cook, uncovered, over a low heat until all the liquid has evaporated (30–45 minutes).

Add 1–2 extra tablespoons butter to the pan, and a grinding of pepper. Shake the carrots, to mix them with the melting butter. Turn into a warmed dish and sprinkle with parsley.

GLAZED CARROTS

Serves 4

150 ml (1/4 pint) water
salt
600 g (1 1/4 lb) young carrots, cut into
  'matchsticks'
2 tbsp butter or margarine
2 tsp light brown sugar
1 tsp lemon juice

Garnish
1 tsp chopped chives
2 tsp chopped parsley

Bring the water to the boil in a pan. Add all the ingredients except the herbs. Half-cover and cook over a medium heat, shaking the pan, until almost all the water has evaporated. Take the pan off the heat, and continue shaking it until the carrots are all coated with glaze. Turn into a warmed dish and sprinkle with the herbs.

WHOLE STEAMED CAULIFLOWER

Serves 4–6

1 medium-sized cauliflower
2 tbsp butter, melted
salt and pepper

Garnish
1 hard-boiled egg yolk, sieved or 1 tbsp
  finely snipped chives and 1 tbsp
  crisply cooked crumbled bacon

Cook the cauliflower stalk side down, in 5 cm (2 in) boiling water for 15–25 minutes until tender when pierced with a skewer. Put the head, again stalk side down, in a warmed serving dish. Pour the melted butter over it, season, and sprinkle with sieved egg yolk or chives and bacon.

CAULIFLOWER AU GRATIN

Serves 4

1 medium-sized cauliflower
40 g (1½ oz) butter or margarine
3 tbsp flour
275 ml (½ pint) milk
100 g (4 oz) grated Cheddar or gruyère
  cheese
salt and pepper

Cook the cauliflower stalk side down, in 5 cm (2 in) boiling water for 15–25 minutes until tender. Place the cooked head, stalk side down, in a warmed oven-proof dish. Make a cheese sauce by melting the butter then stirring in the flour and cooking for 2 minutes. Off the heat, trickle in the milk slowly, stirring constantly. Return to a low heat, bring to the boil, still stirring, and continue stirring until thick. Stir in 75 g (3 oz) of the cheese with the seasoning. As soon as the cheese melts, pour the sauce over the cauliflower. Sprinkle with the remaining cheese, and place under the grill or in a hot oven to brown the top.

Alternatively, steam cauliflower florets over gently boiling water for about 15 minutes, lay them in a shallow dish and coat them with the sauce. Complete the dish as above.

CELERIAC PUREE

*equal quantities of smooth mashed
potato (see page 12) and celeriac
purée (see page 41)
salt and ground black pepper
1/4 tsp grated nutmeg per 450 g (1 lb)
puréed vegetables
softened butter (up to 2 tbsp per 450 g/
1 lb puréed vegetables)
milk or single cream (up to 2 tbsp per
450 g/1 lb puréed vegetables)*

Beat together the mashed potato and celeriac purée until fully blended. Taste the purée and mix in extra potato if needed; a large celeriac root can be strongly flavoured. Season the mixed vegetable purée with salt and pepper and weigh it. Beat in the nutmeg and softened butter to taste. Add milk or cream little by little little (a sloppy purée is unattractive on the plate and difficult to eat). Taste and adjust the seasoning, then cover and reheat gently in a bain-marie or in the top of a double boiler.

Serve as a side dish, as a filling for hollowed tomatoes or as a 'bed' for poached eggs.

BRAISED CELERY

Serves 4

*1 medium-sized head of celery
mirepoix of vegetables (see page 66)
chicken or vegetable stock (see page 65)
25 g (1 oz) butter or margarine
salt and pepper*

Heat the oven to 180°C (350°F) mark 4. Cut the leaf ends of the celery stalks off square and pare the root. String the outer stalks if required. Tie the head in two or three places to hold it in shape. Parboil it in water for 6–8 minutes. Spread the mirepoix in the base of a heavy casserole or oval pot-roaster. Lay the celery on top. Pour in enough stock to cover half the celery, dot the top with the butter and season. Cover tightly with greased greaseproof paper, then with a lid. Cook for 1–1½ hours.

Transfer the celery to a warmed dish; remove the strings and serve with some of the cooking liquid poured over.

BOILED CELERY

Serves 4

4 small tender heads of celery or 2 large ones, halved lengthways
1 tbsp lemon juice
salt and pepper
275 ml (¹/2 pint) coating white sauce or parsley sauce (see pages 63 and 64)

Cut off the leaf ends and leaves, and pare the root ends of the celery. Scrape and string the outside stalks if required. Cut the celery stalks across into 5 cm (2 in) pieces, discarding any immature yellow leaf tips. Bring a pan of water to the boil, add the lemon juice and celery, and cook for 10–20 minutes, depending on the thickness of the pieces, until they are tender. Drain, and season well. Serve coated with white or parsley sauce (see pages 63 and 64).

COURGETTE MEDLEY

Serves 4

2 small onions or 6 spring onions
1 clove garlic
2 tbsp butter or margarine
1 tbsp oil
4 large or 6–8 small courgettes, sliced (5 mm/¹/4 in thick)
2 tomatoes, skinned and sliced
1 tbsp tomato purée
1 tbsp dried basil
3 tbsp white wine or 1 tbsp lemon juice and 2 tbsp water
salt and ground black pepper

Slice the onions thinly and squeeze the garlic over them. In a large frying pan, stir the onion in 1 tablespoon of the butter and the oil for 30 seconds over a low heat. Add the remaining butter and the courgettes, and sauté them for about 3 minutes until they begin to colour. Add all the other ingredients except the seasoning, stir and then cover the pan with a spatter-proof cover or plate. Reduce the heat and cook gently for 8–10 minutes, stirring occasionally, until the courgettes are tender but not mushy. Season to taste before serving.

Cucumber can be cooked in the same way.

SIMMERED FENNEL

Serves 4

4 medium-sized bulbs of Florence
  fennel
2–3 parsley stalks
1 sprig fresh or dried thyme
1 skinned clove garlic (optional)
2 fresh or 1 dried bay leaf
7–8 coriander seeds
6 black peppercorns
4 tbsp olive oil
juice of 1 lemon
275 ml (½ pint) water
salt and pepper

Prepare the fennel by removing the root ends and coarse outer sheaths. Cut off the stem ends and slice them to add to the bouquet garni. Reserve any feathery shoots. Make up the bouquet garni by tying the parsley, thyme, garlic (optional), bay leaf, coriander seeds and peppercorns together in a small square of muslin. Put the olive oil, lemon juice, water, bouquet and salt in a pan; cover, bring slowly to the boil and simmer for 10 minutes. Meanwhile halve or quarter the fennel bulbs, depending on their size. Add them to the pan, and continue cooking until they are tender, about 10 minutes.

Drain the bulbs, reserving the liquid and season to taste. Serve with a little of the liquid poured over to moisten (optional). Garnish with the shredded feathery leaves.

'FRIED' SPRING GREENS

Serves 4

450 g (1 lb) whole heads of young
  spring greens
boiling water
2 tbsp butter
1 tbsp olive oil
good pinch each of salt, pepper, grated
  nutmeg and brown sugar

Bring 2.5 cm (1 in) depth of water to the boil in a pan which will hold the heads side by side. Add the heads and turn them over using two wooden spoons. Cook for 3 minutes or until the leaves soften. Cover the pan, reduce the heat, and simmer for 5 minutes. Drain, reserving the liquid. Lay the heads on a cloth, fold it over them, and squeeze out any free liquid. Cut the heads in half lengthways. Heat the butter and oil in the dry pan, then return 5 mm (¼ in) depth of reserved liquid and the greens. Add the seasonings. Cover, and simmer until the stem ends and ribs are tender, turning occasionally. Drain, or serve with the liquid.

BAKED LETTUCE

Serves 4

1 large firm Webb's lettuce
salt and pepper
2 tsp dried marjoram or oregano
4 spring onions, green and white parts
thinly sliced
6 cm (2½ in) piece of unpeeled
cucumber, diced
4-6 tbsp strong vegetable stock (see
page 65)

Heat the oven to 170°C (325°F) mark 3.
Remove any loose, damaged or wilted leaves or
tips. Wash the lettuce well without breaking it
apart. Cut off the root, and cut the lettuce in
quarters, lengthways. Lay each segment on a
piece of foil large enough to enclose it.
Sprinkle with salt and pepper, and the herbs,
then with the sliced spring onion and
cucumber. Turn up the edges of the foil so that
the liquid cannot run off, and pour the stock
over the segments. Enclose each segment
completely in its foil sheath by folding and
pinching the foil edges over it. Place in a
shallow baking tin and bake for 20–25 minutes
until the lettuce is tender when pierced with a
skewer through the top of the foil parcel.
Unwrap and serve with the liquid in each
parcel.

Cos lettuce or Chinese leaves can be cooked
the same way but will take slightly longer. Cut
away any tough root end or core before
cooking.

STEWED OKRA WITH TOMATOES

Serves 4–6

400 g (14 oz) fresh okra pods
150 ml (¼ pint) vinegar
85 ml (3 fl oz) olive oil
2 large onions, coarsely chopped
8 medium-sized tomatoes, skinned and
chopped
2 tbsp chopped chives
1 tbsp chopped parsley
1 tsp fresh or dried thyme
salt and pepper

Cut off the stems of the okra pods without
cutting into the pods themselves. In a shallow
bowl, marinate the pods in the vinegar for
40 minutes, then drain and rinse them well.
Heat the oil in a pan, add the chopped onions
and stir until browned. Add the tomatoes and
simmer for 5 minutes. Now add the okra pods,
herbs, seasoning to taste and enough hot water
to cover three quarters of the vegetables. Cook
gently, uncovered, for 40–50 minutes, stirring
occasionally.

PETITS POIS A LA FRANCAISE

Serves 4

1/4 lettuce, shredded
6-8 spring onions (bulbs and white stems), sliced
1 sprig each fresh mint and parsley
675 g (1 1/2 lb) small tender fresh peas or frozen petits pois
75 g (3 oz) butter or margarine, melted
pinch of sugar
120 ml (4 fl oz) boiling water
salt and pepper

Put all the ingredients except the seasoning and 25 g (1 oz) of butter or margarine into a pan, in the order given. Cover, and cook gently until the peas are tender, 5–10 minutes (or even less for petits pois). Remove the herbs, season well and add the remaining butter.

PARSNIP PUREE

Serves 4–6

450 g (1 lb) parsnips
2 small carrots
350 g (12 oz) boiled, peeled potatoes
50 g (2 oz) butter or margarine
2-4 tbsp milk
salt and ground black pepper
pinch of grated nutmeg
1-2 tbsp cream (optional)
2 tbsp unsalted butter or chopped parsley to garnish

Wash, peel or scrape and trim the parsnips and carrots. Quarter the parsnips and take out the hard cores. Slice both the parsnips and carrots thinly. Melt half the butter in a heavy pan, add the parsnips and carrots and cook gently for about 6 minutes, turning and tossing the slices. Add the minimum of boiling water and cook for about 20 minutes until soft. Drain thoroughly.

Purée the parsnips, carrots and potatoes together, using a sieve or a food processor. Mix thoroughly, with the remaining butter and some or all of the milk; do not make the purée sloppy. Season well and stir in the cream (optional). Reheat (without boiling) if required. Serve each helping with a dab of butter on top or sprinkled with parsley.

SCALLOPED POTATOES

Serves 4

4 medium-large raw potatoes, peeled and thinly sliced
2 large onions, skinned and thinly sliced
2 tbsp chopped parsley
½ tsp salt
good grinding of black pepper
4 tbsp melted butter or margarine
175 ml (6 fl oz) milk or vegetable stock
(see page 65)

Heat the oven to 190°C (375°F) mark 5. Spread half the potatoes in an even layer about 2.5 cm (1 in) deep in a well-greased shallow baking dish suitable for serving. Spread the onions and half the parsley over the potatoes and season. Cover evenly with the remaining potato slices. Season again and sprinkle with the melted butter. Pour in enough milk or stock to show through the top layer of potatoes. Bake for 1–1¼ hours or until the potatoes are crusty on top and soft underneath. Sprinkle with the remaining parsley.

POTATO RISSOLES

Makes 12–14 rissoles

350 g (12 oz) smooth mashed potato
(see page 12)
1 tsp chopped parsley
50 g (2 oz) cooked minced ham
(optional)
salt and pepper
beaten egg to coat
browned breadcrumbs or Melba toast
crumbs
fat for shallow frying

Cool the mashed potato if freshly made. Mix in the parsley and the ham (optional). Season well. Shape the mixture into balls, then flatten them slightly with your palm. Coat with egg, then with breadcrumbs. Fry in shallow fat, turning once, until golden brown on both sides. Drain on soft kitchen paper, and serve very hot.

Variation
For potato croquettes, use 450 g (1 lb) smooth mashed potato, 25 g (1 oz) butter, 1 tsp parsley and 2 egg yolks for the mixture. Form into cork shapes and coat with egg and breadcrumbs twice, then fry in deep hot oil for 4–5 minutes.

DUCHESSE POTATOES

Serves 4

450 g (1 lb) hot peeled and boiled
  potatoes
50 g (2 oz) butter, softened
1 egg or 2 egg yolks, beaten
salt and pepper
grated nutmeg

Heat the oven to 200°C (400°F) mark 6. Mash the potatoes until very smooth. Beat in the butter and beaten egg or egg yolks, and seasoning. Pipe into rosettes on a greased baking sheet. Bake for about 20 minutes until golden and tipped with brown.

The potato rosettes can be made and refrigerated ahead of time.

BAKED PUMPKIN ON THE SHELL

Serves 4

900 g (2 lb) segment of pumpkin,
  unpeeled
lemon juice
salt and pepper
sprinkling of ground ginger or paprika
2 tsp butter or margarine
chopped parsley to garnish

Heat the oven to 200°C (400°F) mark 6. Cut the segment of pumpkin in half across into two 450 g (1 lb) pieces. These are more convenient to cook than a single long segment and hold any fat or liquid better than small serving portions. Scrape out the seeds and fibre and sprinkle with a little lemon juice. Place the pieces in a greased, shallow baking tin, flesh side up. Sprinkle well with salt and pepper and ginger or paprika. Dot with the butter. Cover with greased foil, tucking it well in around the pumpkin. Bake for 30–40 minutes or until the pumpkin is tender when pierced with a skewer.

To serve, cut each piece in half to make 4 portions. Remove the rind and sprinkle with a little more lemon juice (optional) and with chopped parsley.

SWEETCORN FRITTERS

Serves 4

oil for deep frying
200 g (7 oz) canned sweetcorn kernels,
drained
1 large egg, separated
65 g (2½ oz) flour
½ tsp baking powder
½ tsp salt
pinch of paprika

Set a pan of oil to heat to 185°C (360°F). Mash the kernels with a potato masher or in a food processor. Turn them into a bowl. Beat the egg yolk until thick and stir it into the mashed kernels. Sift together the flour, baking powder, salt and paprika, and stir this dry mixture into the corn in small quantities, blending each in thoroughly. Whisk the egg white until stiff. Stir in one spoonful to lighten the corn mixture, then fold in the rest. Drop small spoonfuls into the hot oil and fry until golden-brown, turning as required. Drain on soft kitchen paper.

Serve at once with grilled ham, roast or fried chicken, or baked stuffed tomatoes.

CORN OYSTERS

Serves 4 (8–10 fritters)

200 g (7 oz) canned sweetcorn kernels,
drained
2 eggs
6 tbsp sifted flour
½ tsp baking powder
⅛ tsp grated nutmeg
salt and pepper
2 tbsp butter or margarine
½ tbsp oil

Mash the sweetcorn kernels with a potato masher or in a food processor. Beat the eggs in a bowl until frothy. Sift in the flour, baking powder, nutmeg and seasoning. Beat well, then fold in the mashed kernels. Heat the butter and oil in a large frying pan. Drop in separately 4 or 5 spoonfuls of the corn batter. Fry until browned underneath, then turn and brown the second sides. Drain on soft paper, then keep warm while frying the remaining batter.

Serve as a side dish with grilled ham or fried chicken, or as a breakfast, brunch or supper dish with grilled bacon.

VEGETABLES AS LIGHT AND MAIN MEALS

A collection of filling and sustaining dishes from
hot stuffed artichokes to spinach soufflé.

HOT STUFFED ARTICHOKES

Serves 4

4 large French globe artichokes
lemon juice
oil
450 g (1 lb) cooked green peas, fresh or
  frozen
a few leaves of fresh mint
salt and pepper
grated nutmeg
275 ml (½ pint) coating white sauce
  (see pages 63 and 64)
1 egg yolk, beaten
1–2 tbsp cream

Trim the tops off the artichokes and neaten the leaf tips and twist off the stalks so that they stand flat. Immerse the artichokes, stem ends down, in gently boiling water adding a little lemon juice and oil to prevent discolouration.

While boiling the artichokes, purée the peas, with the mint leaves and seasonings (in a blender if possible). Make the sauce, or reheat it if made ahead, and beat in the egg yolk and cream. Stir over a very low heat, without boiling, to cook the egg yolk and blend into the purée. Heat the oven to 180°C (350°F) mark 4.

When the artichokes are cooked, an outer leaf should pull off easily (30–50 minutes); turn upside down and drain. Spread out the tops of the artichokes and scoop out the hairy 'choke' with a spoon. Fill the centre with the purée. Wrap each artichoke in foil and reheat in the oven for 12–15 minutes.

MAGGIE'S STUFFED ARTICHOKES

Serves 4

4 large French globe artichokes
shredded smoked salmon trimmings
lemon juice
ground black pepper
425 ml (¾ pint) soured cream

Trim the tops off the artichokes and neaten the leaf tips and twist off the stalks so that they stand level. Immerse in gently boiling salted water, adding a little lemon juice and oil to prevent discolouration. When the artichokes are cooked, an outer leaf should pull off easily (30–50 minutes). Turn upside down and drain; allow to cool completely. Spread out the leaves, removing the small centre cone, and scoop out the hairy 'choke' with a spoon. Season the smoked salmon with lemon juice and ground black pepper to taste. Fill the artichokes with the mixture. The quantity will depend on the size of the artichokes and the shreds. Serve with soured cream.

Variation
For a decorative and cheaper filling, use 2 × 200 g (8 oz) packets of frozen crab sticks. Thaw and chop, then bind with some of the cream or with mayonnaise and use as above.

STUFFED AUBERGINES

Serves 4

2 medium-sized aubergines
salt
3–4 tbsp oil
100 g (4 oz) button mushrooms, finely chopped
1 medium-sized onion, skinned and finely chopped
1 medium-large tomato, skinned and chopped
1 tsp dried basil or thyme
50 g (2 oz) soft white breadcrumbs
1 tbsp chopped parsley
50 g (2 oz) black olives, stoned and chopped
2 tbsp grated Cheddar cheese

Halve the aubergines lengthways, and make criss-cross slits in the cut sides. Sprinkle with salt, and leave, cut side down on a rack for 30 minutes. Brush the cut sides with oil and cook gently under a low grill until tender, turning once. Scoop out most of the flesh, leaving shells 5–10mm (¼–½ in) thick. Reserve the pulp. Heat the oven to 200°C (400°F) mark 6.

Heat 2 tbsp of the remaining oil, and fry the mushroom and onion for 3–5 minutes until soft. Add the tomato and dried herbs. Reserve 2 tbsp of the breadcrumbs and add the rest to the pan with the aubergine pulp, parsley and olives; mix well. Fill the aubergine shells with the mixture. Mix the remaining breadcrumbs and cheese together and use to cover the stuffing. Sprinkle with oil. Place the aubergine halves, cut side up, in an oiled shallow baking-tin. Bake for 15–20 minutes until well heated through and golden on top.

RATATOUILLE

Serves 4–6

3 medium-sized aubergines
salt
2 large onions, skinned and sliced
1 clove garlic, crushed
1 green pepper, seeded and sliced
2–3 courgettes, sliced
4–6 tomatoes, skinned and quartered
75 g (3 oz) margarine
pepper
2 bay leaves
chopped parsley to garnish

Slice the aubergines and sprinkle with salt. Leave for 30 minutes while preparing the other vegetables. Melt the margarine in a pan, add the onions, garlic and sliced pepper. Cover and cook over a low heat for 5 minutes without browning. Drain and dry the aubergine slices and add them to the pan with all the other ingredients except the parsley. Cover and simmer for 30 minutes. Remove the bay leaves. Place in a warmed serving dish, and sprinkle with parsley; or leave, covered, in a cool place until cold.

Serve hot or cold, as a starter, side dish or main dish with rice or pasta.

BEAN SPROUT AND OLIVE STIR-FRY

Serves 2 (as a main dish)

100 g (4 oz) wholemeal pasta shells
2 tbsp corn oil
2 carrots (75 g/3 oz each), coarsely
   chopped
1 sweet red pepper, deseeded and
   coarsely chopped
2 large shallots, thinly sliced
100 g (4 oz) button mushrooms, sliced
100 g (4 oz) garden peas
175 g (6 oz) bean sprouts
10 black or green olives, drained,
   stoned and chopped
50 ml (2 fl oz) vegetable stock (see page
   65)
1 tbsp soy sauce
1 tbsp dry sherry
chopped parsley to garnish

Cook the pasta shells in fast-boiling water for 5–6 minutes or until tender. Drain and set to one side. Heat the oil in a wok or large frying pan. Add the carrots, pepper and shallots and stir over a medium-high heat for 3 minutes or until the pepper and shallot soften. Add the sliced mushrooms and stir for 2 minutes. Stir in the peas and bean sprouts, and stir for another 2 minutes to soften the bean sprouts. Mix in the pasta and olives and stir. Mix the liquids together and pour into the pan. Simmer for 2 minutes, stirring, to moisten the dish. Serve sprinkled with chopped parsley.

CAULIFLOWER FRITTERS

Serves 4

225 g (8 oz) flour
1 tsp salt
2 tbsp oil
225 ml (8 fl oz) milk and water mixed
oil for deep frying
600 g (1¼ lb) small cauliflower florets
3 egg whites

Make a coating batter by sifting together the flour and salt into a bowl and making a hollow in the centre. Put in the oil, and a little of the liquid. Stir in the flour little by little, while adding the remaining liquid gradually, then beat the batter mixture briskly until smooth. Chill until the florets are ready. Set a pan of oil to heat to 180°C (350°F).

Parboil the florets for 4 minutes, then drain and dry them thoroughly. Whisk the egg whites until stiff. Give the batter mixture a last beat, thinning it with a little more water if necessary, and fold in the egg whites. Dip the florets one by one in the batter and fry them in small batches in the hot oil, turning them as needed. Remove them with a slotted spoon when golden-brown and drain on kitchen paper. Serve with hollandaise sauce (see page 65).

MIXED VEGETABLE STIR-FRY

Serves 4

225 g (8 oz) small cauliflower florets
1 yellow or red sweet pepper, deseeded
    and cut into small strips
3 tbsp oil
100 g (4 oz) onion, finely chopped
2 small carrots, coarsely grated
6 tbsp vegetable stock (see page 65)
salt and ground black pepper
2 small courgettes, coarsely grated
25 g (1 oz) flaked almonds
2 tbsp dry sherry
1 tbsp tomato juice
450 g (1 lb) freshly cooked or reheated
    brown rice

Steam the cauliflower florets and strips of pepper over boiling water for 5 minutes. Heat half the oil in a wok or deep frying pan with a spatter-proof cover. Add the onion and fry until soft. Add the remaining oil, cauliflower florets, pepper strips and grated carrot. Stir over a fairly high heat for 3 minutes. Add the stock, reduce the heat and cover the pan. Cook gently for 4 minutes, stirring twice. Season and stir in the courgettes and all the remaining ingredients except the rice. Stir, uncovered, for 2 minutes, mixing the ingredients well. Serve with the brown rice.

CHICORY ROLLS

Serves 4

8 medium-sized heads of chicory with
    yellow leaf–tips
juice of ½ lemon
pinch of salt
8 slices cooked ham, large enough to
    enclose chicory heads
butter or margarine
275 ml (½ pint) coating white sauce
    (see pages 63 and 64)
25 g (1 oz) grated cheese

Choose chicory heads about the same size.
Trim the root ends, then gouge out the centre
cores. Remove any discoloured leaves; rinse.
Put the heads into a pan of boiling water, and
blanch for 5 minutes to reduce the bitter taste;
drain. Bring the minimum of fresh water to the
boil, add the lemon juice and salt and the
chicory. Cook until the heads are tender,
12–20 minutes. Drain, and cool slightly on a
board, then gently squeeze out excess
moisture. Heat the oven to 180°C (350°F)
mark 4.

    Spread one side of each ham slice with
butter. Lay a chicory head on the spread side
of each slice; wrap the ham around the
chicory. Arrange the rolls in one layer in a
greased, shallow baking-dish suitable for
serving. Cover with the white sauce, sprinkle
with cheese and bake for 7–10 minutes.

BRAISED CHINESE LEAVES

Serves 4

Chinese leaves (900 g/2 lb head)
2 slices cooked ham, shredded
mirepoix of vegetables (see page 66)
beef, chicken or vegetable stock)
    (see page 65)

Garnish
1 egg yolk, hard-boiled (optional)
chopped parsley (optional)

Trim the root end of the head and remove any
discoloured leaves or leaf tips. Wash the head
and dry it. Split from the top and almost to the
root, carefully take out the crinkly pale heart
and fill the space with the ham. Reshape the
head and tie it tightly in two or three places.
Parboil it for 5 minutes, then drain. Spread the
mirepoix in the bottom of a heavy flame-proof
casserole. Lay the head on top and pour in
enough stock to cover half of it. Cover it with
greased foil or greaseproof paper, then with a
lid. Cook gently for 50–60 minutes on top of
the stove or in the oven at 180°C (350°F)
mark 4.

Place the head on a serving dish and remove the string. Either boil down 150 ml (¼ pint) of the stock until syrupy and pour it over the cabbage, or top with crumbled hard-boiled egg yolk and chopped parsley.

SPRING LOAF

Serves 4–6

2 small carrots
1 medium-sized onion
1 tbsp oil
350 g (12 oz) cooked spring greens or
    summer cabbage, chopped
½ tsp each fresh thyme and
    marjoram, chopped or ¼ tsp
    dried herbs
6 eggs
½ tsp salt
flaked butter or margarine

Heat the oven to 180°C (350°F) mark 4. Grate the carrot and onion coarsely. Heat the oil and stir the grated vegetables in it for 2 minutes. Turn them into a bowl and mix in the chopped greens and herbs. Beat the eggs lightly and fold them in with the salt.

Grease or line and grease a 450 g (1 lb) loaf tin. Turn in the mixture, and dot with flaked butter. Bake for 40 minutes.

Serve hot, or cool in the tin for slicing cold. The loaf shrinks as it cools.

LEEKS A LA GRECQUE

Serves 4 (as a starter)

450 g (1 lb) leeks
175 ml (6 fl oz) water
2 tbsp lemon juice
2 fresh bay leaves or 1 dried leaf
½ tsp coriander seeds, crushed
1 sprig fresh thyme or ¼ tsp dried
    thyme
1 clove garlic, crushed
salt and pepper
400 g (14 oz) tomatoes, skinned and
    chopped

Cut off the roots of the leeks and green leaf tops and slice them. Put all the other ingredients except the tomatoes into a pan, and bring gently to the boil. Add the tomatoes and simmer gently, uncovered, for 20 minutes. Add the sliced leeks for the last 5–6 minutes. Serve hot, or cool in the sauce and serve cold.

POOR MAN'S GOOSE

Serves 4–6

1 medium-sized marrow (about 1 kg/
  2¼ lb)
100 g (4 oz) margarine, softened
1 large onion, peeled
1 celery stalk
100 g (4 oz) cracked wheat
150 ml (¼ pint) strong vegetable stock
  (see page 65)
150 ml (¼ pint) dry still cider or apple
  juice
salt and pepper
1 cooking apple (about 175 g/6 oz)
6–8 fresh sage leaves, chopped or ½ tsp
  dried sage
50 g (2 oz) seedless raisins

Wash the marrow, split it lengthways and remove the seeds and fibre. Prick the skin of both halves with a knife point in several places, and brush the hollows with a little of the margarine. Chop the onion and celery finely. Melt 50 g (2 oz) of the margarine in a large deep frying pan and fry the onion and celery until soft. Add the cracked wheat, stock and cider or juice with a little seasoning. Bring slowly to simmering point, cover and simmer for 15 minutes. While simmering, peel, core and chop the apple. When the cracked wheat is cooked, add the apple, sage and raisins. Mix well and leave until cool enough to handle. Heat the oven to 190°C (375°F) mark 5.

Fill both marrow halves with the mixture. Reshape the marrow or bake the two halves separately.

Put the re-shaped marrow or both halves (cut side up) in a baking tin. Roll any remaining stuffing into forcemeat balls and add them to the tin. Dot the tops of the marrow halves or the top skin of a reshaped marrow with margarine and add any left over to the tin.

Cover the dish loosely with greased foil. Bake for 1–1½ hours; the marrow should be tender but not mushy. Baste with the margarine two or three times while baking. Uncover the tin for the last 20 minutes to brown the marrow, baste well, then complete the cooking. Serve with apple sauce.

GREEN VEGETABLE CURRY

Serves 4–6

275 ml (½ pint) boiling water
100 g (4 oz) desiccated coconut
2 tsp ground coriander
¼ tsp each ground cumin and ginger
pinch each of ground cinnamon and
    cloves
⅓ tsp chilli powder
⅓ tsp turmeric
75 g (3 oz) shredded cabbage
100 g (4 oz) green peas, shelled
100 g (4 oz) green beans, sliced
225 g (8 oz) potatoes, peeled and diced
3 tbsp corn oil
2 medium-sized onions, chopped
50 g (2 oz) green pepper, deseeded and
    chopped
¼–½ tsp salt
2 tsp lemon juice

The coconut milk should be made, and the spices mixed well ahead. Make the coconut milk by pouring the boiling water over the desiccated coconut. Leave for 2 hours. Process both the coconut and liquid in an electric blender for 30 seconds. Strain through a cloth-lined sieve, and squeeze the residue in the cloth to extract all the milk. Mix all the spices together. Set to one side.

Put the cabbage, peas, beans and diced potatoes into 275 ml (½ pint) boiling water in a pan. Reduce the heat, simmer for 5 minutes and drain. Heat the oil in a second pan, add the onions and stir until beginning to brown. Add the pepper and spices and stir round. Add the simmered vegetables, season with salt and cook for 4 minutes, stirring once or twice. Add the coconut milk and lemon juice, and cook gently until the vegetables are tender.

JACKET POTATOES WITH CHEESE

Serves 4

2 large baking potatoes
1 tbsp oil
120 ml (4 fl oz) natural yoghurt
2 tbsp finely snipped chives
1 tsp salt
a few grains of cayenne pepper
4 tbsp grated Cheddar cheese
paprika

Heat the oven to 200°C (400°F) mark 6. Scrub the potatoes well and pat dry. Brush with oil. Place on a baking sheet and bake for 45–75 minutes, depending on size, until soft when pierced with a thin skewer. Cool just enough to handle. Cut the potatoes in half lengthways, and scoop out most of the flesh with a spoon, leaving a 5 mm (¼ in) shell. Mash the flesh in a bowl or beat with an electric beater, adding the yoghurt gradually. Blend well, then add the chives and seasoning to taste. Pile the mixture back in the shells. Sprinkle with the cheese mixed with a sprinkling of paprika. Reduce the oven heat to 180°C (350°F) mark 4 and bake for 10–15 minutes or until the cheese is melted and potatoes are hot.

STUFFED GREEN PEPPERS

Serves 4

2 large green peppers
1 tbsp oil
40 g (1½ oz) onion, finely chopped
40 g (1½ oz) celery, finely chopped
75 g (3 oz) carrot, grated or finely
  chopped
175 g (6 oz) cooked haricot beans,
  finely chopped
75 g (3 oz) tomato, chopped coarsely
¼ tsp salt
grinding of black pepper
pinch of dried thyme
good pinch of dried basil
3 sprigs parsley, chopped
150 ml (¼ pint) tomato juice
4 tbsp cheese, coarsely grated

Rinse the peppers, cut off the stalks and halve the fruit lengthways. Take out the cores, seeds and inside ribs. Put the halves in a pan of boiling water, bring back to the boil and leave to stand off the heat while making the stuffing. Heat the oven to 180°C (350°F) mark 4.

Heat the oil in a fairly large frying pan, add the onion and celery, and stir over a low heat until golden brown. Add the carrot and continue stirring until just tender. Stir in the beans, tomato, seasoning and dried herbs and simmer, stirring, for 5–6 minutes until well blended. Take off the heat. Stir in the parsley. Leave to stand while draining the peppers.

Place the pepper halves, cut side up, in a shallow baking dish. Season inside and fill with the stuffing. Pour the tomato juice into the dish around (not over) the peppers. Cover the dish with greased foil. Bake for 30 minutes or until pepper halves are tender. Uncover, and top the pepper halves with cheese. Return to the oven, uncovered, for 5 minutes to brown the cheese.

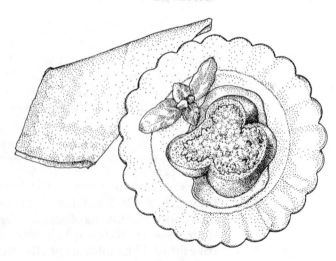

SPINACH ROULADE

Serves 4

450 g (1 lb) cooked spinach, chopped
1 tbsp butter or margarine, softened
4 eggs, separated
1 tbsp plain flour
3 tbsp grated Cheddar cheese
salt and pepper to taste

Filling
15 g (1/2 oz) butter
175 g (6 oz) mushrooms
275 ml (1/2 pint) white sauce (thick
  coating consistency, see page 63

Heat the oven to 190°C (375°F) mark 5. Prepare a 20 × 33 cm (8 × 13 in) Swiss roll tin by greasing and lining with baking parchment. Grease the parchment lightly.

Drain the chopped spinach in a nylon strainer. Cream the butter in a bowl by beating with an electric or rotary beater. Beat in the egg yolks until well blended. Sprinkle with the flour, cheese and seasoning and beat them in, followed by the spinach. In a separate bowl, whisk the egg whites until stiff, then fold them into the mixture.

Spread the spinach mixture gently and evenly over the prepared Swiss roll tin. Bake for 15 minutes or until the spinach mixture is firm.

Meanwhile make the filling by melting the butter and gently cooking the mushrooms; drain. Heat through the white sauce and add the mushrooms.

Place a sheet of greased baking parchment, greased side down over the tin. Holding the parchment and tin together, turn them over, and lay on a flat surface. Lift off the tin, and carefully peel off the lining parchment.

Spread the spinach mixture with the filling, then roll it up like a Swiss roll from one short end. An easy way to do this is to lift the parchment under one end so that the end curls over, then use a palette knife to ease it gently into a scroll. Serve at once if possible; the roll solidifies as it cools; although still good even when cooled and reheated, it is not quite as delicious.

Variations
The roulade can also be stuffed with fish in a thick cream sauce; any stuffing mix; asparagus tips with prawn and cheese sauce.

SPINACH SOUFFLE

Serves 6

450 g (1 lb) fresh spinach
2 tbsp onion, grated
75 g (3 oz) butter, softened
pinch of grated nutmeg
3 tbsp flour
275 ml (½ pint) milk
100 g (4 oz) full-fat soft cheese
pinch of paprika
salt and pepper
4 eggs, separated

Remove the stalks and any coarse ribs from the spinach. Cook it in very little, if any, water until tender. Drain, then squeeze as dry as possible. Chop it, then mash, pound or process it in a food processor until smooth. Cook the grated onion gently in 4 teaspoons of the butter until soft, and mix it into the spinach purée with the nutmeg. Heat the oven to 190°C (375°F) mark 5.

Grease a 750-ml (1½-pint) soufflé dish with a little butter. Melt the remaining butter over a low heat. Stir in the flour and cook, stirring, for 2 minutes, without letting the flour colour. Pour in the milk gradually, stirring constantly, and continue stirring until the sauce thickens. Add the cheese by spoonfuls and stir until melted and blended. Then stir in the spinach purée, a small pinch of paprika and seasoning to taste. Take off the heat and cool for 5 minutes. Meanwhile beat the egg yolks until liquid. Beat them into the spinach mixture.

Whisk the egg whites until stiff but not dry. Stir 1 tablespoon into the spinach panada. Fold in the rest lightly. Turn the mixture gently into the soufflé dish. Bake for 25 to 30 minutes. Serve immediately.

STUFFED TOMATOES

Serves 4

1 aubergine (about 275 g/10 oz)
¹/₂ tsp salt
8 firm tomatoes (about 100 g/4 oz
  each)
1 tbsp butter or margarine, softened
1 large egg, beaten
25 g (1 oz) onion, finely chopped
1 tsp dried thyme
salt and black pepper
6 tbsp grated Cheshire cheese
8 tbsp soft white breadcrumbs

Peel the aubergine and slice it into rounds. Immediately put them into a pan, add the salt and pour in 2.5 cm (1 in) depth of boiling water. Cover tightly, bring back to the boil and cook until soft. While cooking, cut the tops off the tomatoes, scoop out the seeds and juice and turn upside down to drain. Heat the oven to 190°C (375°F) mark 5.

Drain the aubergine slices. Mash them or blend in a food processor with the butter, egg, onion, thyme, seasoning and 3 tablespoons of the cheese. Add enough breadcrumbs to make a stuffing which is soft but not sloppy.

Season the tomato cases lightly inside and fill with the mixture. Place cut side up in a greased, shallow baking tin or dish, cover loosely with greased foil, and bake for 25 minutes. Uncover, sprinkle with the remaining cheese and bake for a further 5 minutes or until the cheese is melted and the tomatoes are soft.

BASIC SAUCES, STOCKS AND SAVOURY BUTTERS

A collection of basic sauces, stocks and flavoured
butters which complement any vegetable.

WHITE SAUCE (ROUX METHOD)

Makes 275 ml (½ pint)

Pouring consistency
20 g (¾ oz) butter or margarine
2 level tbsp plain flour
275 ml (½ pint) milk or milk and
vegetable-flavoured liquid
small pinch of grated nutmeg
(optional)
salt and pepper

Melt the butter and sprinkle in the flour, stir until smooth. Cook over a gentle heat for 2–3 minutes until the roux bubbles. Remove from the heat and add the milk gradually, stirring continuously to make sure that it is all absorbed smoothly. Bring the sauce to the boil, still stirring, especially around the base of the pan. When the sauce thickens, simmer for 1–2 minutes, then remove from the heat, and season to taste.

The sauce can be made ahead; press damped or greased greaseproof paper over it to prevent a skin forming. Reheat when required.

Variations
(1) Coating consistency. Use 25 g (1 oz) butter and 3 tablespoons flour.
(2) Thick coating consistency. Use 40 g (1½ oz) butter and 4 tablespoons of flour. Use for vol-au-vent filling.
(3) Binding consistency or panada. Use 50 g (2 oz) butter and 50 g (2 oz) of flour. This is used mainly for fritters and croquettes or as the basis of a vegetable soufflé.
(4) Cream sauce. Stir in 1 beaten egg yolk and 1 tablespoon of single or double cream into the completed sauce (any consistency); reheat without boiling.

These variations also apply to white sauce made by the all-in-one method (see page 64).

WHITE SAUCE (ALL-IN-ONE METHOD)

Makes 275 ml (½ pint)

20 g (¾ oz) softened butter or soft tub
    margarine
2 level tbsp plain flour
275 ml (½ pint) milk or milk and
    vegetable flavoured liquid
small pinch nutmeg (optional)
salt and pepper

Put all the ingredients together in a pan and whisk over a medium heat until the sauce comes to the boil and thickens. Continue cooking for 2–3 minutes.

Variations
(1) Parsley sauce. Add 1–2 tablespoons of chopped parsley to 275 ml (½ pint) of white sauce made with milk, with a squeeze of lemon juice (optional).
(2) Mushroom sauce. Lightly fry 50–75 g sliced button mushrooms in a knob of butter until soft but not coloured. Drain and fold them into 275 ml (½ pint) white sauce made with milk. Season with nutmeg, salt and pepper.
(3) White onion sauce. Simmer two medium-sized onions, skinned and chopped, in lightly salted water until soft. Drain well, reserving the liquid. Make 275 ml (½ pint) white sauce, using half milk and half the onion cooking liquid. Fold the onions into the completed sauce with the grated rind of half a small lemon (optional). Season to taste.
(4) Cheese sauce. Add 50–100 g (2–4 oz) grated Cheddar or similar cheese, a pinch of dry mustard, salt and cayenne pepper to the freshly made hot white sauce; stir until melted and reheat if needed without boiling.

These variations also apply to white sauce made by the roux method (see page 63).

HOLLANDAISE SAUCE

Makes 225 ml (8 fl oz)

175 g (6 oz) softened butter
3 tbsp white wine vinegar
1 fresh bay leaf or ¹/₂ dried leaf
6 black peppercorns
3 egg yolks
2 tbsp water
salt and pepper

Melt and then cool the butter. Boil the vinegar, bay leaf and peppercorns in a small pan until reduced to 1 tablespoon. Strain into a heat-proof bowl; discard the flavourings. Beat the egg yolks with the water and then with the reduced vinegar until frothy. Place the bowl over a pan of simmering water and continue beating until the sauce thickens. Gradually beat in the butter, beating each addition in thoroughly. The sauce should be thick and shiny and served while lukewarm, so leave in a bain-marie until serving time.

VEGETABLE STOCK

Makes 1.75 litres (3 pints)

¹/₂ clove garlic
4 medium tomatoes, quartered
5 small onions, skinned and halved
5 medium carrots, halved
3 small celery stalks, cut in 2 cm (³/₄ in)
    pieces
6–8 parsley stalks
2 litres (3¹/₂ pints) water

Squeeze the garlic over the tomatoes. Put all the ingredients in a large pan, making sure that the water covers the solids. Bring to the boil. Reduce the heat, cover, and simmer for 1 hour.

Leave to stand off the heat for 30 minutes. Strain through muslin into a suitable container. Cool by standing the container in chilled water until cold. Use the same day if not refrigerated. Chill, covered, for 2 days only, or freeze for up to 2 months.

BROWN VEGETABLE STOCK

Makes about 2 litres (3½ pints)

25 g (1 oz) margarine
3 small onions with skins on, quartered
3 medium-sized carrots, sliced
2 outside stalks celery, sliced
2 tomatoes, sliced
6 parsley stalks
½ dried bay leaf or 1 fresh leaf
6 black peppercorns
1 whole blade mace
lemon juice to taste
2 litres (3½ pints) boiling water
salt to taste

Heat the margarine in a stew-pan. Add the onions, carrots and celery and stir-fry until the vegetables are lightly browned. Add all the remaining ingredients except the salt. Bring to the boil. Reduce the heat, cover and simmer for 1 hour. Leave to stand off the heat for 20 minutes. Strain through damp butter-muslin into a bowl. Season. Cool completely, then remove any fat from the surface. Chill for 2 days or freeze for up to 2 months.

MIREPOIX OF VEGETABLES

Makes a 'bed' for braising 4 celery heads

2 tsp butter or margarine
2 tsp frying oil
25 g (1 oz) rindless bacon, diced
1 onion, skinned and chopped
1 carrot, scraped and chopped
1 celery stick, thinly sliced
2 shallots, skinned and chopped (optional)
vegetable stock (see page 65)

Heat the butter and oil in a pan. Add the bacon and vegetables, cover and cook gently for 10 minutes, stirring occasionally. Add enough stock to cover the vegetables. Place the food to be braised on top. Cover the pan tightly and simmer until the braised meat or vegetable is cooked; baste occasionally with the liquid.

A mirepoix of mixed chopped vegetables is used as a 'bed' when braising meat or other vegetables such as celery or cos lettuce. It can also be used as a side dish or garnishing vegetable in its own right, or as the basis of a puréed soup.

GREEN BUTTER

2–3 tsp parsley, finely chopped
½ tbsp lemon juice
anchovy essence
50 g (2 oz) slightly salted butter,
softened

Beat the parsley, lemon juice and a few drops of anchovy essence into the butter.

Variations
(1) Curry butter. Beat ½ teaspoon of curry powder, ¼ teaspoon of lemon juice, ground black pepper and salt to taste into 50 g (2 oz) slightly salted softened butter.
(2) Garlic butter. Beat ¼–½ a clove of minced garlic with salt to taste into 50 g (2 oz) slightly salted, softened butter.
(3) Herb butter. Beat 1 teaspoon of finely chopped fresh herb leaves with salt to taste into 50 g (2 oz) slightly salted, softened butter.
(4) Maitre d'Hotel butter. Beat three finely chopped sprigs of blanched parsley with a few drops of lemon juice, white pepper and salt to taste into 50 g (2 oz) slightly salted, softened butter.

SALADS

SALADS AS SIDE DISHES

Assorted combinations of vegetables and fruits
with tasty dressings.

MIXED BEAN AND CORN SALAD

Serves 4

175 g (6 oz) cooked French or runner
*   beans, sliced into small pieces*
200 g (7 oz) each drained, cooked or
*   canned cannellini beans, red kidney*
*   beans and sweetcorn kernels*
2 small inside stalks celery, finely
*   chopped (optional)*
1/2 medium-sized onion, finely chopped
2 tbsp Walnut dressing (see page 91)

Mix all the ingredients in a bowl, and toss with the dressing. Serve at room temperature.

BROCCOLI AND PASTA SALAD

Serves 4

75 g (3 oz) fresh broccoli spears
75 g (3 oz) French beans
75 g (3 oz) cooked pasta spirals,
*   drained and cooled*
2 spring onion bulbs with white stems,
*   sliced*
50 g (2 oz) black olives, stoned and
*   chopped*
2 cocktail gherkins, chopped

Dressing
2 tsp dry whole grain mustard
1 tbsp lemon juice
3 tbsp oil

Cut off the broccoli stems. Break the heads into small florets, and peel and slice the stems if tender. Top and tail the beans, and cut diagonally into small lengths. Cook the vegetables together until just tender, drain and cool. Mix with the pasta, spring onions, olives and gherkins in a salad bowl. Whisk together the dressing ingredients and sprinkle over the salad.

BEETROOT WITH YOGHURT DRESSING

Serves 4

6 medium-sized beetroot, cooked
225 ml (8 fl oz) French dressing with
    lemon (see page 89)
150 ml (¼ pint) natural yoghurt
green tops of 3 medium-sized spring
    onions, finely sliced

Skin the beetroots and slice them. Put them in a bowl with the French dressing and leave for several hours. When ready to serve, whisk the yoghurt until liquid and stir in the spring onion tops. Pour any free dressing off the beetroot and pour the yoghurt mixture over it.

CALABRESE SALAD

Serves 4–6

175 g (6 oz) small cauliflower florets
175 g (6 oz) calabrese heads cut into
    small florets
125 g (4 oz) young carrots, thinly sliced
125 g (4 oz) green beans, sliced
2 small courgettes, thinly sliced

Marinade
6 tbsp soya oil
6 tbsp cider vinegar
3 tbsp lemon juice
pinch of sugar
½ tbsp grated onion
½ tsp dry mustard
½ garlic clove, squeezed
½ tsp oregano

Steam the cauliflower, calabrese, carrot and beans over simmering water for 9 minutes. Drain, mix at once with the courgette slices and cool. Meanwhile mix together all the marinade ingredients in a jar with a secure stopper. Shake the marinade vigorously to blend. Put the partly-cooled vegetables in a bowl and pour the marinade over them. Toss lightly; cover and refrigerate for several hours, stirring occasionally. Drain off any free marinade before serving.

CARROT AND ORANGE SALAD

Serves 4

350 g (12 oz) carrots
2 medium-sized oranges
50 g (2 oz) raisins
1 tbsp French dressing (see page 89)
good grinding of black pepper

Top, tail and scrape the carrots and grate them. Blanch and peel the oranges, and cut the flesh into segments removing the pith, membrane and pips. Cut the segments in half across and mix with the grated carrots. Add the raisins and mix. Moisten the salad with the French dressing and grind black pepper over it before serving.

Variations
Add 2 tablespoons of finely snipped chives to the salad. For a salad with a sharper flavour to accompany game birds or pork, substitute 2 tablespoons of drained capers for the raisins.

CAULIFLOWER SALAD

Serves 4

1 medium-sized cauliflower
salt and white pepper
vinaigrette dressing (see page 90)

Divide the cauliflower head into small sprigs, and cook in boiling water for 5 minutes. Drain well, season lightly, and toss with the dressing in a bowl while still hot. Cool completely, turning the sprigs over occasionally. Pour off any free liquid before serving.

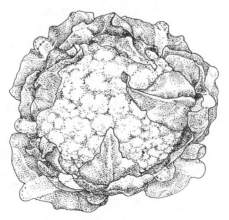

COLESLAW

Serves 4–6

450 g (1 lb) firm white cabbage
3 medium-sized carrots
1 sharp eating apple
1 tbsp lemon juice
25 g (1 oz) seedless raisins
salt and freshly ground black pepper
150 ml (¼ pint) mayonnaise (see page
  92) or mayonnaise and natural
  yoghurt mixed

Remove any discoloured leaves and core the cabbage; shred it finely. Top, tail and scrape the carrots and grate them coarsely. Quarter, core and dice the apple, toss the dice at once with the lemon juice, and mix with the cabbage and carrot. Add the raisins. Season well, then bind with the mayonnaise or mayonnaise and yoghurt.

CELERY AND FENNEL SALAD

Serves 4

Garnish
3 tbsp sesame seeds
25 g (1 oz) walnut pieces

Salad
2 fennel bulbs with feathery shoots
6 medium-sized celery stalks
2 small courgettes

Dressing
4 tbsp lemon juice
1 tsp dry mustard
2 tsp clear honey
6 tbsp corn or sunflower oil

For the garnish, scatter the sesame seeds on a baking sheet, and toast in the oven at 180°C (350°F) mark 4 for 15 minutes, stirring twice while toasting; the seeds should be light gold. Chop the walnuts finely and mix with the seeds.

To make the salad, snip off the feathery fennel shoots and set to one side. Take off any stubs of stem and coarse outside sheaths and pare the root ends. Quarter the bulbs lengthways and blanch in boiling water for 2 minutes; drain and cool. Trim the tops and root ends of the celery stalks and string if necessary. Cut off the ends of the courgettes.

Slice the celery thinly. Slice the fennel and courgettes lengthways and cut into small strips. Mix the vegetables in a salad bowl.

Make the dressing by whisking the lemon juice, mustard and honey in another bowl, and gradually whisking in the oil. Pour enough of the dressing over the salad to moisten it well. Scatter the sesame-walnut garnish over the salad. Snip the feathery fennel shoots, and sprinkle on top.

CELERY AND APPLE SALAD

Serves 4

2 red-skinned dessert apples
2 tbsp lemon juice
100 g (4 oz) inside celery stalks,
    trimmed and finely sliced
50 g (2 oz) sultanas
4 cocktail gherkins, thinly sliced

Dressing
4 tbsp natural yoghurt
4 tbsp mayonnaise (see page 92)
1 tsp clear honey
lettuce leaves (optional)

Quarter, core and dice the apples. Coat at once with the lemon juice. Mix the apple dice, celery, sultanas and gherkins in a salad bowl. Whisk together the yoghurt dressing ingredients, then toss the salad in it with your preferred dressing. Make a 'bed' of lettuce leaves on a platter and pile the salad on top or serve it in individual bowls.

Serve as a side salad with curries or barbecued meats or as a starter with yoghurt dressing.

French dressing (see page 89) may be substituted for yoghurt dressing.

CELERIAC REMOULADE

Serves 4

450 g (1 lb) celeriac
2 tsp salt
2 tsp lemon juice
4 tbsp Dijon mustard
3 tbsp boiling water
120 ml (4 fl oz) olive oil
2 tbsp white wine vinegar
chopped parsley to garnish

Peel the celeriac and shred it coarsely. Mix with the salt and lemon juice and leave to stand for about 30 minutes. Rinse well under running water and dry with soft kitchen paper.

Put the mustard in a warmed, dry mixing bowl. Whisk in the water gradually, with an electric beater if possible. Then whisk in the oil drop by drop at first as for mayonnaise; add enough to make a thick, creamy sauce. Whisk in the vinegar. Fold in the celeriac, cover and refrigerate overnight. Sprinkle with parsley just before serving.

This classic salad is most often served alone as a starter, but it can also be used as a winter side salad, with cold turkey or game meat. The mustard dressing must not be confused with the mayonnaise-based remoulade sauce served with grilled meats or fish.

CHICORY SALAD

Serves 4

4 medium-sized heads of chicory
4 small inside celery stalks

Dressing
1 large egg yolk
1/4 tsp made English mustard
salt and pepper
1 tbsp corn oil
1 tbsp double cream
1 tbsp white wine vinegar
1/4 tsp dried dill leaves

Wash the chicory and celery stalks and dry in a cloth. Cut off the root ends of both. Gouge out the bitter cores of the chicory heads, and remove any celery leaves. Slice both vegetables and mix in a bowl.

To make the dressing, whisk the egg yolk in a small bowl with the mustard and seasoning. Whisk in the oil drop by drop as for mayonnaise. When it thickens slightly, add the cream and whisk in the vinegar little by little with the dried dill. Pour the dressing over the salad ingredients.

CUCUMBER SALAD

Serves 4

1 large cucumber
salt and white pepper
3 tbsp French dressing (see page 89)
2 tsp fresh mint leaves, finely chopped

Slice the cucumber thinly into a shallow bowl. Season lightly. Mix the dressing with the mint leaves and pour over the cucumber. Chill, covered, for 30 minutes. Drain off any free liquid before serving.

MINTED CUCUMBER SALAD

Serves 4

1 small cucumber
salt
1 garlic clove
150 ml (1/4 pint) natural yoghurt
1 tbsp olive oil
1 tbsp finely chopped fresh mint

Cut off the ends of the cucumber, and shred the rest coarsely. Spread on a plate and sprinkle well with salt. Leave for 30 minutes. Meanwhile, squeeze the garlic into the yoghurt, add the oil and whisk to blend them. Add half the mint. Drain, rinse and dry the cucumber and mix with the dressing. Taste before serving and add a little extra salt if you wish. Serve sprinkled with the remaining mint.

MELON AND CUCUMBER SALAD

Serves 4

1 large orange
½ medium-sized cucumber
½ small honeydew melon
1 tbsp fresh mint, finely chopped
1 tsp white wine vinegar
pinch of salt
½ tsp clear honey
lemon juice

Put the orange in boiling water for 1–2 minutes, turning it over once. Drain. Holding it in a cloth, peel it and cut the flesh into segments, remove the pith, membrane and pips. Cut the segments in half across and put in a salad bowl. Cut the unpeeled cucumber into 1 cm (½ in) dice, and jumble them with the orange. Quarter the melon, discarding any seeds, and cut the flesh free from the rind; then cut it into 1 cm (½ in) cubes. Mix the cubes into the salad with the mint. Stir the remaining ingredients together, using lemon juice and water to adjust the flavour of the dressing; it should be tangy. Sprinkle the dressing over the salad, and toss to coat it.

Serve with chaufroid of chicken, a cold fish mousse and similar dishes.

Mint vinegar can be used, either bought or home-made (see page 93) instead of wine vinegar.

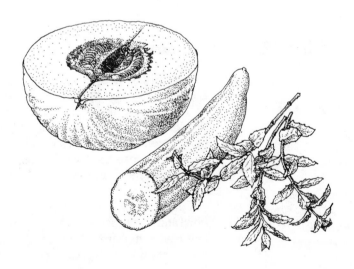

PEPPER AND CUCUMBER SALAD

Serves 4

2 sweet red peppers
1 large mild onion
10 cm (4 in) piece of cucumber
a few drops of soy sauce
lemon juice
6 tbsp natural yoghurt

Cut off the tops of the peppers, and remove the cores and seeds. Peel the onion and chop it finely. Slice both the peppers and cucumber thinly, and arrange them in overlapping circles on a platter. Sprinkle with the onion. Mix enough soy sauce and lemon juice into the yoghurt to give it a spicy flavour. Pour it over the salad and serve at once.

POTATO SALAD WITH DILL

Serves 4–6

6 large new potatoes or waxy old
    potatoes
120 ml (4 fl oz) French dressing with
    lemon (see page 89)
2–3 tbsp chopped parsley
2 tbsp finely snipped fresh dill leaves
salt and pepper

Steam the potatoes in their skins until just tender. Cool just enough to handle and then scrape off the skins. Cut the potatoes into 1 cm (½ in) dice. Put in a bowl, add the French dressing and herbs, and toss together lightly. Season to taste. Cool thoroughly, turning over once or twice while cooling. Drain off any excess dressing before serving.

SPINACH SALAD WITH BACON

Serves 4

225 g (8 oz) young spinach leaves
1 tbsp chives, finely snipped
pinch of paprika
pinch of salt
1 thick slice wholemeal bread without
    crusts
garlic oil for frying (see page 91)
4 rashers rindless streaky bacon
French dressing (see page 89)

Wash and dry the spinach leaves, and tear them into bite-sized pieces. Mix with the chives, paprika and salt. Cut the bread into dice and fry in a little garlic oil until crisp and lightly scented. Drain on soft paper. Add the bacon to the pan and fry until crisp. Drain on soft paper, and crumble finely. Mix with the spinach.

Put the bread cubes in the bottom of a salad bowl and pile the spinach salad on top. Just before serving, sprinkle or toss the salad with a few drops of French dressing.

TOMATO SALAD

Serves 4

6–8 medium-sized tomatoes
1 tbsp olive oil
½ tsp white wine vinegar or cider
    vinegar
2 large spring onion bulbs, thinly sliced
salt and freshly ground black pepper
fresh or dried basil or thyme leaves

Slice the tomatoes thinly. Lay them in overlapping rings in a shallow bowl or on a serving plate. Sprinkle well with the oil and vinegar. Separate the spring onion slices into rings and scatter them over the dressed tomato slices. Season well, and sprinkle the herb leaves on top.

TOMATO-MOZZARELLA SALAD

Serves 4

400 g (14 oz) firm tomatoes
100 g (4 oz) mozzarella cheese, thinly
    sliced
salt and freshly ground black pepper
1 tbsp finely snipped chives
½ tbsp walnut oil (see page 91)

Discarding the ends, slice the tomatoes into thin rounds. Arrange them in overlapping rings on a flat plate. Cover with the cheese slices. Season lightly with salt and pepper and sprinkle with the chives and walnut oil. Serve at room temperature.

This salad makes a good starter.

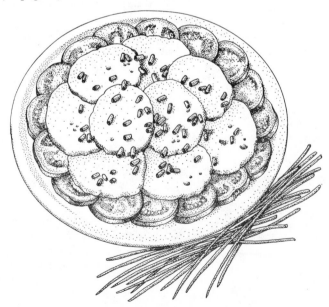

WATERCRESS AND MUSHROOM SALAD

Serves 4

225 g (8 oz) button mushrooms, thinly
　sliced
50 g (2 oz) watercress leaves
1–2 tsp chopped parsley
2 tsp finely snipped chives
French dressing made with tarragon
　vinegar (see page 89)

Mix together the mushrooms, watercress,
parsley and chives. Sprinkle with the French
dressing just before serving.

ITALIAN SALAD

Serves 4–6

1 head curly endive
75 g (3 oz) radiccio
50 g (2 oz) button mushrooms, sliced
½ green pepper, cut across, deseeded
　and cut into thin rings
½ medium-sized courgette, thinly
　sliced
salt and black pepper
1 tbsp pine nut kernels
sprinkling of lemon juice

Dressing
350 g (12 oz) tomatoes
1 tbsp grated onion
salt and black pepper
½ tsp lemon juice (for very ripe
　tomatoes)
2 tbsp olive oil
chopped fresh basil

Separate the endive stalks and rinse well, then
pat dry. Use the outer leaves to line a salad
bowl. Tear the small centre leaves into pieces.
Shred the radiccio, removing any core. Mix
the torn endive leaves, radiccio, mushrooms,
pepper rings and courgette slices, season and
turn into the lined bowl. Sprinkle with the
pine nuts and lemon juice. Serve the dressing
separately.

For the dressing, scald and skin the
tomatoes. Chop them roughly, then process
for ½ minute in an electric blender with the
onion, seasoning, lemon juice if used and oil.
Stir well just before serving, and sprinkle with
basil.

SIMPLE GREEN SALAD

Serves 4

1 small round lettuce
1 small bunch watercress
mustard and cress
4 medium-sized spring onions, green
   and white parts
6 cm (2½ in) piece cucumber, unpeeled
1–2 tbsp chopped fresh mixed herbs as
   available (e.g. parsley, tarragon,
   thyme, hyssop, marjoram, rue,
   sweet cicely, savory)
French dressing with lemon (see page
   89)

Remove the roots and any damaged or
discoloured leaves from the lettuce and
watercress. Separate the lettuce leaves and
take the watercress leaves off the stems. Cut off
the stems of the cress. Rinse the leaves under
running water and shake or toss them in a salad
basket or cloth to dry. Tear the lettuce into
small pieces, chop any large watercress leaves
and slice spring onions finely. Dice the
cucumber. Mix all the leafy ingredients lightly
in a bowl with the onion, cucumber and
chopped herbs. Just before serving, toss with
the dressing.

   If fresh herbs are not available, add one or
two chapons (see page 93) to the salad bowl
and remove just before serving.

SALADS AS LIGHT
AND MAIN-COURSE
DISHES

A collection of more elaborate salads containing
vegetables, fruit and also some form of protein.

ANTIPASTO MISTO

Serves 4

2 hard-boiled eggs
1½ tbsp olive oil
½ tbsp white wine vinegar
1 tbsp finely chopped chives
1 tbsp finely chopped celery
½ tbsp chopped parsley
salt and ground black pepper
150 g (5 oz) small ripe tomatoes with
    ends removed, sliced
1 tbsp grated raw onion
4 thin slices Parma ham
2 slices Mortadella sausage
1 medium-sized fennel bulb with
    outside sheaths removed, cut in thin
    strips
1 tbsp French dressing with ½ tsp
    dried rosemary added
2 tbsp drained capers

Slice the eggs. Make a dressing by mixing the oil, vinegar, chives, celery, parsley, salt and pepper together; pour over the eggs. Cover the tomato slices with the onion. Roll up each slice of ham loosely. Remove any skin off the Mortadella, cut the slices into small thin strips and season with black pepper. Blanch the fennel strips for 2 minutes in boiling water and drain. Mix with the French dressing, and cool.

Place the eggs with their dressing in a strip across the centre of an oblong or oval platter about 20 cm (8 in) wide and 28 cm (11 in) long. Place the tomato slices in a row alongside the egg on one side and arrange the ham rolls alongside the tomato. On the other side, place the Mortadella, then the fennel. Sprinkle the whole dish with capers.

SAVOURY RICE SALAD

Serves 4

100 g (4 oz) shelled green peas
25 g (1 oz) Parma or Westphalian
    ham
36 cooked shelled prawns
275 g (10 oz) cooked brown rice
salt and white pepper
good pinch of grated nutmeg
2 tbsp olive oil
2–3 tsp lemon juice
2 tbsp chopped parsley

Cook the peas in unsalted water until almost tender. Cut the ham into thin short strips and add it to the pan. Cook for 1 minute longer. Drain and cool. Mix in the prawns.

Toss the rice to separate the grains. Mix together all the remaining ingredients to make a dressing, reserving some parsley for garnishing. Mix the dressing with the rice, then fold in the peas, ham and prawns. Garnish with the reserved parsley.

SALADE NICOISE

Serves 4

large flat green lettuce leaves
200 g (7 oz) can of tuna in oil, drained
2 hard-boiled eggs cut in segments
salt and ground black peppr
4 medium-sized tomatoes, skinned and
  sliced
4 tbsp finely chopped onion
4 tbsp finely sliced cooked celery
1 green pepper, deseeded and cut into
  small thin strips
50 g (1¾ oz) can anchovy fillets,
  drained
8 black olives, stoned
French dressing (page 89)
pinch each of dried rosemary and basil

Make a 'bed' of lettuce leaves on a large flat platter. Chop the tuna roughly and place it with the egg segments in a level layer in the centre of the 'bed'. Season all the vegetables and arrange them in a ring around the tuna and egg. Split the anchovy fillets lengthways and lay in a lattice pattern on the dish, with the olives in the spaces between the fillets.

Serve with French dressing with the herbs mixed in.

SPAGHETTI SALAD WITH TUNA

Serves 6

225 g (8 oz) spaghetti
salt
2 × 200 g (7 oz) cans tuna in oil
400 g (14 oz) green peppers (2 large
  peppers)
275 g (10 oz) firm tomatoes
150 g (5 oz) onions

Dressing
reserved oil from cans of tuna
120 ml (4 fl oz) mayonnaise (see page
  92)
3 tbsp milk
4–5 drops Tabasco
1 tbsp soy sauce
2 tsp tomato ketchup
salt and black pepper
pinch of white sugar
good pinch of paprika

Break the spaghetti into 7.5 cm (3 in) lengths and cook it in lightly salted water until just tender. Drain and cool. Meanwhile, drain the tuna, reserving the oil. Split the peppers, remove the cores, seeds and inside ribs and cut the flesh into small thin strips. Skin and quarter the tomatoes, remove the seeds, cores and pulp and dice the flesh. Skin and shred the onions.

Whisk the reserved oil with the other dressing ingredients, seasoning well; the flavour should be spicy. Flake the tuna coarsely, and mix it with the spaghetti, most of the pepper strips and all the tomato and onion. Toss with the dressing. Chill, covered, for 30 minutes. Turn the salad onto a shallow serving platter and garnish with the reserved pepper strips.

SMOKED MACKEREL SALAD

Serves 4

8 medium-sized new potatoes
225 g (8 oz) cooked, cooled French
　beans
4 small tomatoes
2 eggs, hard-boiled
225 g (8 oz) skinned smoked mackerel
　fillet
4 large lettuce leaves
2–3 tbsp French dressing with lemon
　(see page 89)

Boil the potatoes in their skins and cool. While cooling, top and tail the French beans and cut diagonally into 2.5 cm (1 in) lengths. Quarter the tomatoes and eggs. Cut the fish into small pieces.

Lay the lettuce leaves in a 'bed' on a flat platter. Scrape the skins off the potatoes and cut them into small cubes. Arrange the potato cubes, beans, tomatoes, eggs and fish on the lettuce. Sprinkle the salad with dressing.

MANGETOUT AND PASTA SALAD

Serves 4–6

225 g (8 oz) green noodles
120 ml (4 fl oz) mayonnaise (see page
　92)
1 garlic clove, squeezed
2 tbsp white wine vinegar
2 medium-sized courgettes
225 g (8 oz) mangetout, topped and
　tailed
100 g (4 oz) button mushrooms, sliced
175 g (6 oz) cherry tomatoes, cut in half
1 tbsp finely chopped parsley
1 tbsp finely chopped fresh mint

Cook the noodles in boiling water until just tender. Drain and put in a bowl. Mix together the mayonnaise, garlic and vinegar, and toss the mixture with the noodles. Set to one side. Cut off the ends of the courgettes and split in half lengthways, then slice across thinly into half-moons. Slice the mangetout into strips diagonally if large. Put both vegetables in a round-bottomed sieve or strainer and dip in boiling water for a few seconds, then toss to dry them. Add to the noodles with the mushrooms and halved tomatoes. Sprinkle with the herbs, and chill until needed. Bring back to room temperature to serve.

Variation
Substitute 50 ml (2 fl oz) soured cream for half the mayonnaise.

CURRIED BEAN AND EGG SALAD

Serves 4

600 g (1¼ lb) drained, cooked butter
  beans or 2 × 450 g (16 fl oz) cans
salt and pepper
3 tbsp vegetable oil
2 medium-sized onions
2 tsp curry powder
120 ml (4 fl oz) hot water
50 ml (2 fl oz) soured cream
4 hard-boiled eggs, shelled
paprika for sprinkling

Season the drained beans with salt and pepper.
Chop the onions. Heat the oil in a pan and fry
the onions until beginning to colour, stirring
constantly. Mix in the curry powder
thoroughly, then stir in the beans. Continue
stirring for 1 minute. Add the water and
simmer for 3 minutes or until the water has
almost evaporated. Mix in the soured cream.
Turn half the beans into a bowl. Cut the eggs
in half and place on top of the beans, then
cover with the rest of the beans. Cool
completely. Sprinkle with paprika before
serving.

TOMATO, CELERY AND CHEESE SALAD

Serves 4

5 medium-sized tomatoes, skinned
4 medium-sized stalks celery
1 × 200 g (7 oz) can sweetcorn kernels,
  drained
225 g (8 oz) Cheddar cheese, finely
  diced
4 tbsp mayonnaise (see page 92)
lettuce leaves (from a round lettuce)
25 g (1 oz) chopped walnuts
1 tsp grated orange rind
walnut halves or watercress sprigs to
  garnish

Quarter the tomatoes lengthways. Put four
quarters to one side. Scrape out the seeds and
pulp of the rest and cut the flesh into small
pieces. Top and tail the celery stalks, string if
needed and slice finely. Mix the celery,
sweetcorn and cheese with the tomato pieces
and toss lightly with the mayonnaise. Make a
'bed' of lettuce leaves on a flat platter and pile
the salad on top. Sprinkle with chopped nuts
and orange rind. Garnish the centre of the
salad with the four reserved tomato quarters,
skinned side up, arranged like flower petals.
Place the walnut halves or tiny sprigs of
watercress around the edge of the salad.

ROYAL TURKEY SALAD

Serves 4

150 ml (¼ pint) soured cream
1 tbsp cress, chopped
salt and pepper
pinch of white sugar
½ tsp French mustard
350 g (12 oz) cold cooked brown turkey
meat without skin
3 medium-sized tomatoes, quartered
10 cm (4 in) piece cucumber, unpeeled
3 large or 4 small spring onions, green
and white parts with roots and leaf-
tips removed
1 egg yolk, hard-boiled

Mix together the soured cream, cress, seasoning, sugar and mustard in a bowl which will hold all the turkey meat. Dice the turkey and mix it with the dressing. Pile the mixture in the centre of a flat salad plate. Remove the seeds and pulp of the tomatoes. Chop the tomato flesh and cucumber, not too finely, and slice the spring onions. Mix these three ingredients together and season well. Place them in a ring around the edge of the turkey salad. Sieve the hard-boiled egg yolk over the turkey.

CHICKEN, HAM AND FRUIT SALAD

Serves 4

225 g (8 oz) cold cooked chicken meat
without skin
100 g (4 oz) cold cooked ham in one
thick slice
225 g (8 oz) cold, cooked new potatoes
1 medium-sized sharp eating apple
3 tbsp cider vinegar
100 g (4 oz) fresh ripe red plums
salt and pepper
pinch of dry mustard
¼ tsp caster sugar
2 tbsp sunflower oil
½ small Webb's lettuce, shredded

Dice both the meats. Scrape the skins off the new potatoes and dice. Mix all three in a bowl. Peel, core and dice the apple and toss in the vinegar. Halve, stone and chop the plums. Pour the vinegar off the apples into a bowl, and mix in the seasoning, mustard and sugar. Whisk in the oil slowly. Add the fruits and a little shredded lettuce to the meat and potato, and toss with the dressing. Spread the remaining lettuce on a flat platter, pile the salad on top and serve at once.

CHEF'S SALAD

Serves 4

4 large cos lettuce leaves
1 tbsp French dressing (see page 89)
75 g (3 oz) cold cooked turkey meat
*   without skin*
75 g (3 oz) cold cooked ham in one
*   thick slice*
75 g (3 oz) cold cooked tongue in one
*   thick slice*
75 g (3 oz) gruyère cheese
chopped parsley to garnish

Wash, dry and shred the lettuce, and toss with just enough dressing to moisten it. Place it in the bottom of a salad bowl. Cut all the meats and the cheese into small strips and jumble them on top of the lettuce. Sprinkle with any remaining dressing and garnish with chopped parsley.

MOULDED PARTY SALAD

Serves 4

1 large open-hearted lettuce
4–6 large round slices pressed tongue
6–7 medium-sized tomatoes, skinned
*   and sliced*
150 g (5 oz) Edam cheese, thinly sliced
*   without rind*
3 hard-boiled eggs, quartered
sliced gherkins
blue cheese dressing (see page 90) or
*   soured cream*

Separate the lettuce leaves and rinse and dry them carefully. Lay one medium-sized leaf in the bottom of a 1-litre (2-pint) pudding basin. Cover it with a slice of tongue. Cover this with another lettuce leaf, then put in a layer of tomato slices, another lettuce leaf and a layer of sliced cheese. Repeat the layers until all the ingredients are used, separating them with lettuce. The top layer should also be lettuce. Cover with a round of greaseproof paper, then put a small plate and a heavy weight on top. Chill for at least 1 hour.

Shortly before serving, shred any remaining lettuce. Drain off any free liquid on top of the pressed salad. Unmould it onto a serving platter. Arrange the lettuce round it, with the eggs and sliced gherkins on top. Spoon the dressing over the salad.

Variation
The salad is also delicious made with 150 g (5 oz) thinly sliced smoked salmon instead of tongue.

WALDORF SALAD

Serves 4

4 red skinned eating apples
2–3 tbsp lemon juice
1 tsp caster sugar
150ml (¼ pint) mayonnaise (see page 92)
1 head celery with outside stalks removed
50 g (2 oz) walnuts
lettuce leaves

Wash the apples, quarter and core them; leave them unpeeled. Dice them, and toss the dice at once with the lemon juice, sugar and 1 tablespoon of the mayonnaise. Set to to one side. Trim the root and leaf ends of the celery stalks, and slice finely. Set aside a few perfect nuts for garnishing and chop the remainder. Just before serving, combine the celery, chopped nuts and remaining mayonnaise with the apples and add to a salad bowl lined with lettuce leaves. Garnish with the whole nuts.

DRESSINGS, OILS AND VINEGARS

Light oil and vinegar dressings for tender-leafed
green salads and creamy, spicy or mayonnaise-
based dressings to go with crisp or more strongly
flavoured vegetables.

FRENCH DRESSING

Makes about 50 ml (2 fl oz)

2–3 tbsp corn or other light oil
pinch of dry mustard powder
pinch of sugar
salt and pepper
1 tbsp wine vinegar or 2 tsp vinegar
and 1 tsp lemon juice

Mix the oil with the seasonings in a bowl. Stir or beat in the vinegar, or vinegar and juice, drop by drop until an emulsion forms. Stir or beat again just before use.

Alternatively, shake the oil and seasonings in a securely stoppered jar, add the vinegar, stopper the jar and shake vigorously. Repeat just before use.

Use any pure light oil (not a blended one). Olive oil is too heavy for dressing delicate green salad leaves. Malt vinegar is also generally too strong. Both are best kept for dressing strongly flavoured vegetables and leaves such as chicory or endive. A dressing for fruits is best made partly with lemon juice.

FRENCH DRESSING WITH LEMON

Makes 120 ml (4 fl oz)

5 tbsp corn or other light oil
salt to taste
1 tbsp wine vinegar
2 tbsp strained fresh lemon juice
white pepper (freshly ground if
possible)
pinch of sugar

Try to make the dressing not more than ½ hour before use. Whisk the oil and salt together in a bowl (try just a sprinkling of salt at first). Add the vinegar and lemon juice, then grind in the pepper, add the sugar and whisk for a full 30 seconds. Pour the dressing into a jar with a secure stopper. Shake the jar hard for 10–20 seconds before sprinkling it on the salad.

Variation
For French dressing with herbs, add 1 tablespoon mixed fresh herbs (e.g. finely snipped chervil, chives, tarragon) to the dressing when whisking, or for a tomato flavoured dressing add ½ teaspoon of tomato purée when whisking.

VINAIGRETTE DRESSING

Makes 100 ml (3 fl oz)

2–3 tbsp corn or groundnut oil
pinch of dry mustard
salt and black pepper
1 tbsp white wine vinegar
1/2 tsp finely chopped chives
1/2 tsp finely chopped parsley
1/2 tsp finely chopped fresh dill,
   tarragon or chervil
1 tsp finely chopped capers
1 tsp finely chopped pitted green olives
   or gherkin

Mix the oil and seasonings and stir or beat in the vinegar drop by drop until an emulsion forms. Add the flavourings, mix well, and leave to stand for 1–2 hours before use.

THOUSAND ISLAND DRESSING

Makes about 175 ml (6 fl oz)

120 ml (4 fl oz) mayonnaise (see page 92)
1 tbsp chilli sauce
1/2 tbsp finely chopped chives
1/2 tbsp finely chopped green olives
1 tbsp finely chopped canned pimiento
1 tbsp tomato ketchup
1/2 tsp white wine vinegar
1/2 tsp paprika

Beat all the ingredients together until well blended.

There are many versions of this classic American dressing. This spicy mayonnaise would be good over hard-boiled eggs or diced cooked potatoes.

BLUE CHEESE DRESSING

Makes about 150 ml (1/4 pint)

40 g (1 1/2 oz) blue cheese without rind
120 ml (4 fl oz) soured cream
1 tbsp lemon juice
1 large spring onion bulb, finely chopped

Sieve the cheese into a bowl. Work in the soured cream and lemon juice little by little until the mixture is smooth. Add the onion. Pour into a jar with a screw-topped lid. Close and shake well. Chill for 2 hours.

Shake again just before use. Pour over cucumber or tomato salad, or a plain white cabbage slaw.

WALNUT DRESSING

Makes about 95 ml (3½ fl oz)

1½ tbsp white wine vinegar
½ tbsp French Dijon mustard
1 tsp clear honey
50 ml (2 fl oz) walnut oil

Whisk together the vinegar and mustard until blended, then whisk in the honey and oil. Turn into a jar with a secure stopper and close. Shake vigorously just before use.

Use on strongly flavoured green leaf or herb salads.

GARLIC OIL

Makes 275 ml (½ pint)

275 ml (½ pint) pure corn or
*   groundnut oil*
3–4 cloves garlic

Put the oil and garlic cloves in a bottle or jar with a flat, screw-on top. Put in a cool place, standing on a saucer. Invert the bottle every day for 10 days; do not shake it.

Use to make salad dressings or for frying bread dice to make garlic-flavoured chapons (see page 93)

Variation
For tarragon or thyme oil, wash 2–4 sprigs of the herb, blot dry and place in the oil instead of garlic cloves. For lemon oil, put in a wide strip of thin yellow rind and omit the garlic.

MAYONNAISE

Makes 350 ml (12 fl oz)

275 ml (½ pint) corn or soya oil
3 egg yolks
1 tbsp white wine vinegar or lemon
  juice
½ tsp salt
¼ tsp dry mustard

Bring all the ingredients to room temperature. Warm the oil slightly until just tepid. Rinse a mixing bowl in hot water and dry it thoroughly. Put in the egg yolks and beat for 2 minutes or until the yolks thicken. Add the vinegar or lemon juice, salt and mustard, and beat for another half minute. Still beating, add the oil drop by drop until the liquid in the bowl thickens. Occasionally beat without adding extra oil to make sure that all the oil is being absorbed. When the mixture thickens, add the oil a little more quickly, but continue beating constantly until the mayonnaise thickens or all the oil has been added. To prevent the mayonnaise curdling, beat in 1 tablespoon boiling water at the end. Beat in extra seasoning to taste.

If the mayonnaise separates, beat 1 tablespoon of mayonnaise into 1 teaspoon of made mustard in a clear, warmed bowl. Beat until the mayonnaise thickens. Repeat the process, adding the mayonnaise in small spoonfuls.

Store completed mayonnaise in a tightly covered container in the refrigerator.

Olive oil can be used but it is heavy and slightly more difficult to mix in smoothly than a lighter oil. Use a flavoured oil such as garlic oil, or a herb-flavoured vinegar as a variation. Puréed spinach and fresh herbs can be added to make 'green' mayonnaise.

TARRAGON VINEGAR

Makes 700 ml (1¼ pints)

2 fresh tarragon sprigs
700 ml (1¼ pints) white wine vinegar

Leave the tarragon in a dark place for 4 to 5 days. Put it in a wide-necked clear glass jar with a vinegar-proof seal with the vinegar for 2 to 3 weeks. Take out the sprays and add a few sprigs of fresh herbs; stopper securely.

Use the same method for making other herb vinegars such as basil, mint or thyme vinegar.

CHAPONS

1 slice of toast or dry bread
1 clove of garlic
garlic oil for frying (optional)

Cut the toast or bread into 3 cm (1 in) squares. Rub with the cut side of the raw garlic clove. Alternatively, fry the squares in garlic oil (see page 91).

Chapons added to the bottom of the salad bowl and removed before serving leave only a faint almost indefinable aroma of garlic on the salad ingredients. Chapons are ideal where only a hint of garlic is required.

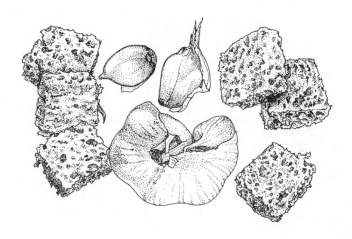

WHAT IS THE WI?

If you have enjoyed this book, the chances are that you would enjoy belonging to the largest women's organisation in the country — the Women's Institutes.

We are friendly, go-ahead, like-minded women, who derive enormous satisfaction from all the movement has to offer. This list is long — you can make new friends, have fun and companionship, visit new places, develop new skills, take part in community services, fight local campaigns, become a WI market producer, and play an active role in an organisation which has a national voice.

The WI is the only women's organisation in the country which owns an adult education establishment. At Denman College, you can take a course in anything from car maintenance to paper sculpture, from book-binding to yoga, or cordon bleu cookery to fly-fishing.

All you need to do to join is write to us here at the **National Federation of Women's Institutes, 39 Eccleston Street, London SW1W 9NT,** or telephone 01-730 7212, and we will put you in touch with WIs in your immediate locality. We hope to hear from you.

ABOUT THE AUTHOR

Maggie Black has been writing about cookery for many years. Her career in this field began when she joined Ward Lock Ltd to edit *Mrs Beeton's Cookery and Household Management*. Since then she has written about smoking foods, barbecuing and, in particular, the folklore of food and traditional dishes. Recently, she has been working on cooking for health, especially for elderly people, concentrating on vegetable cookery and lighter meals. She is the author of *The WI Book of Soups and Starters*.

INDEX